FIONNUALA O CONNOR was born in Belfast. She regularly provides political analysis for radio and television documentaries and is the *Economist*'s Northern Ireland Correspondent. Her book, *In Search of a State: Catholics in Northern Ireland* (Blackstaff Press, 1993), won the Christopher Ewart-Biggs Memorial Prize and the Orwell Prize. A second book, *Breaking the Bonds: Making Peace in Northern Ireland*, was published in April 2002 by Mainstream.

A Shared Childhood

The story of the integrated schools
in Northern Ireland

FIONNUALA O CONNOR

THE
BLACKSTAFF
PRESS

INTEGRATED EDUCATION FUND

First published in 2002 by
Blackstaff Press Limited
Wildflower Way, Apollo Road
Belfast BT12 6TA

in association with

The Integrated Education Fund

© Fionnuala O Connor, 2002

Fionnuala O Connor has asserted her right under the Copyright, Designs and
Patents Act 1988 to be identified as the author of this work.

Typeset by Techniset Typesetters, Newton-le-Willows, Merseyside

Printed in Ireland by Betaprint

A CIP catalogue record for this book is available
from the British Library

ISBN 0-85640-725-9

www.blackstaffpress.com
www.ief.org.uk

Contents

Introduction

The story of Northern Ireland's integrated schools – schools specifically planned to educate together the children of Catholics, Protestants, of all faiths and none – is now more than twenty years old. It is in large part a record of endeavour – tireless, costly and continuing – by idealistic and often brave individuals. In a dysfunctional and divided society, where many cannot recognise the failings of their own groups and where schooling touches the fundamental issue of identity, it is also a story of muddled motives among both friends and enemies, and of considerable opposition, all the more difficult to overcome because it is often disguised.

A Shared Childhood became the title of this work because that is the experience most of those involved hope integrated education can provide. The aim of this book is to explain the course of developments to date and to outline debate on the future, to highlight the positive in the story, and to identify the negative and put it in context. The book is built on information and insights from around forty interviews with parents, teachers, other staff, governors, pupils and pioneers, some of whom have played several roles simultaneously, plus the opinions of friends, enemies and observers, primarily educationalists.

What came to be known as 'integrated education', or simply 'integration', has been described as a movement, the schools it produced as a 'sector'. These are terms that some involved do not entirely accept, but they are used even by the hostile. It seems remarkable to outsiders that there could be hostility to the idea of providing, in the teeth of often bitter segregation, the experience through integrated education of at least a shared childhood. A look at the first twenty years of integration reveals as much about the society from which it emerged, however, as about those who set it up and maintain it, and those who praise and blame become more understandable. Successive Northern Ireland Office ministers have shown considerable sympathy for the idea. The pioneers have been lavishly praised, especially, it sometimes seems, by the outside world. Those at home who are less than starstruck by what is now a significant, though still small corner of educational provision, are not all mean-spirited segregationists.

Some think that integrated education is essential to communal reconciliation. Political development spurred by the Good Friday Agreement is still at an early stage, but common sense alone suggests that structures and institutions shared by strongly antagonistic politicians will not diminish prejudice and build trust, unless there are complementary efforts in the wider community. The Agreement said that promoting tolerance was an essential aspect of reconciliation, singling out 'initiatives to facilitate and encourage integrated education'. But the future for integration, as for Northern Ireland, remains unclear. The sub-text and implications of change since the Agreement are nowhere more remarkable than in the outcome to date for integrated schools. Many in the sector, to the lasting surprise of some of them, now regard Martin McGuinness, once an Irish Republican Army (IRA) leader, as a friend because of his policies as Sinn Féin minister for education, and would be apprehensive about his replacement, say, by a

Democratic Unionist Party (DUP) minister after the 2003 Stormont election. Reorganisation of secondary education, as encouraged by Mr McGuinness to dispense with selection through the eleven-plus examination, will if carried through, have major implications for integrated schools. Some see the prospect as a threat, others as an opportunity.

The Integrated Education Fund (IEF) commissioned this book with a grant from the Wates Foundation, in the hope that it would spark debate on the way forward at a crucial moment, and that it might also serve as a handbook for the curious and for potential customers – parents. An editorial committee accepted a structure which was to draw largely on personal accounts and be a readable narrative, rather than an academic study or a chronology. They agreed stoically at the outset that the writer's judgement would be final, and they have honoured that agreement without complaint. Individual committee members also offered their own experiences and unstinting helpful advice.

Between them, the interviewees quoted report views from most of the schools begun from scratch, plus a number of 'transforming' schools, as well as opinions from outside the sector. The spread of views includes urban and rural schools, primary and secondary, situated east, west, north and south. A large number of opinions overlapped or were almost identical: I have tried to include as many voices as possible. Schools described, some named and others not for reasons which will be explained, are those where practice and experience provided illustration of central issues or provoked useful discussion.

Public figures like DUP education spokesman Sammy Wilson, and Sinn Féin's Martin McGuinness, were happy to speak on the record, but a considerable number of interviewees preferred anonymity. For many, the choice of integrated education was and still is a business fraught with difficulties, opening family, and in some cases communal, rifts. The twenty-year history of the sector has included internal difficulty as well as public controversy. Many were willing to be identified on particular topics but not on others. Most parents and pupils, many teachers, other staff and governors, and external figures, spoke freely but in confidence, which meant removing identifying details. In some cases the speakers and schools are disguised, I hope inoffensively, by fudging descriptions or changing factual details like place. Words are, however, quoted as spoken or written. Initial face-to-face and phone conversations were occasionally refreshed or continued by email. It would have been courteous to name the schools which offered a welcome and to chart their histories, but that would not have made for a readable overview, with enough detail to make the sector's development comprehensible and to suggest the shape of the future. I hope few will feel that strong feelings in the school they know best have been neglected.

Most interviews date from the years 2000–2002, though several accounts draw on notes made as far back as 1985. These I preserved for family as well as journalistic reasons, since I am a political journalist but also a parent, Catholic in origin and married to a Protestant. Both of us helped to set up an integrated primary school in 1985 (Forge, Belfast). For some time I was secretary in that founding group, and our two daughters were educated, very happily, in the sector.

I would like to acknowledge the openness and generosity of the liaison team set up by the IEF and the Northern Ireland Council for Integrated Education (NICIE): Brian Lambkin, Anne Odling-Smee, Jan O'Neill, Colm Murray-Cavanagh, and Frances Donnelly, NICIE senior development officer. NICIE staff led by Michael Wardlow (chief executive) were always helpful and informative. Any errors that survive input and advice from those named are entirely my responsibility. I am also grateful to Pat Harper, who edited the book, and to all the team at Blackstaff Press. My husband David McVea read drafts with his customary forbearance and made many useful suggestions. I owe him as always.

Glossary

TYPES OF SCHOOL MANAGEMENT

CONTROLLED

Controlled schools (often called 'state' or Protestant schools, effectively Protestant in management and largely Protestant in staffing and enrolment) are managed by ELBs through boards of governors which include parents, teachers and representatives of Protestant churches. Funded 100 per cent by government.

VOLUNTARY (MAINTAINED)

Maintained schools (usually called Catholic schools or Catholic maintained schools) are managed by boards of governors which consist of members nominated by Church trustees, along with representatives of parents, teachers and ELBs. Funded 100 per cent by government.

VOLUNTARY (NON-MAINTAINED)

These are mainly grammar schools, managed by boards of governors which consist of persons appointed as provided in each school's scheme of management, along with representatives of parents and teachers and, in most cases, members appointed by DENI or ELBs. Significantly funded by government.

GRANT-MAINTAINED INTEGRATED SCHOOLS

These are so called when integrated schools are recognised as viable and grant-aided by official funding. They are under the control and management of a board of governors, which employs the teachers and is tasked to ensure that the management, control and ethos of the schools are likely to attract equal numbers of Protestant and Catholic pupils. Of a total of sixteen governors, at least six must be parents.

CONTROLLED INTEGRATED SCHOOLS

These are also managed by a board of governors but the relevant ELB treats it like any other controlled school and employs the teachers. Four parents are entitled to sit on the board of governors of a CIS, compared with two in an ordinary controlled school and six in a GMI.

INDEPENDENT SCHOOLS

In addition to the public system of free education, there are also independent schools. These schools do not necessarily follow the Northern Ireland curriculum and do not receive grant aid from DENI. Some of these schools charge fees which are payable directly to the school by parents. Independent schools receive no grant aid from government. Integrated schools are termed independent before being recognised as viable and receiving their first official funding.

1
Parents and Pioneers

Why did they do it? Those who set up the first planned integrated school in 1981, Lagan College, and three more in Belfast four years later, were far from being a coherent group or even groups but they had a strong connecting thread. At its simplest, many of them wanted something for their children that had not been available to them, which is perhaps the most common parental dream the world over. 'Integrated' parents say the same thing repeatedly, individuals spontaneously echoing the words of others with identical passion: 'When I was a kid I never met a Catholic/ Protestant. I met my first Catholic/Protestant when I was in my twenties. I never knew a Protestant/Catholic to speak to until I grew up.' Given the almost total separation of Northern Ireland's education systems and the segregation of much of society, such experiences are common and frequently lamented. Regret is often heightened by awareness of the individual's inability to make any significant change to their separated surroundings or way of life. In choosing integrated schools for their children, many feel that they are rowing against a ceaseless tide.

At an early meeting, in 1984, of a group of parents who would eventually establish an integrated primary school, Forge, in south Belfast, one of the two first primaries, a very young mother spoke with difficulty about her ambitions for it. She had already begun, cautiously, to make friends with several in the group. 'I've never in my life said anything in public,' she said, her voice shaking with nerves. 'All I ever knew about Catholics is they're Taigs and they hate us, and my ma and da and all belonging to them were scared of them. But between the lot of us we didn't know a single Taig to speak to. Where we live there's none, it's all the one sort. That's not what I want for my children.'

How could anyone fail to support efforts to educate children together? No one can easily propose that Northern Ireland's children should be brought up separately; as an educationalist who has given discreet but steadfast support for years says: 'once you say that, it is plainly wrong.' History and politics, the origins of the sector, the make-up of those who launched it, some of the rhetoric that has accompanied its growth and, perhaps least often, the performance of the forty-seven primary and second-level integrated schools all help explain what might otherwise seem irrational opposition. By contrast, it has been easy to understand why parents in a divided place, themselves educated separately, very often living and sometimes working in wholly segregated surroundings, should have had a yearning and at times a burning need to make schooling into something that provided a shared childhood. It was perhaps especially understandable during the worst years of the three-decade long Troubles, the years with the highest death tolls which followed the upheavals in politics and society of 1969 and 1970. People involved in the first wave of founding groups as parents and teachers or helpers and supporters in various ways, are insistent, and remarkably unanimous, about what motivated them in that traumatic period. Many had escaped Northern Ireland for a while, then returned determined to do better for the next generation.

'I came back after living in England, of all years in 1972 (the year with the highest death toll). It was awful – car-bombs, deaths and more deaths. When All Children Together [ACT] started, I went along sort of in despair ... You went away and came back wanting it to be different for your kids, when you had them ... The two of us went to university in England, married there and came back. It was a conscious decision for me that I'd never teach in a school that was Catholic. It took me long enough dealing with the guilt and all that. But I didn't want a typical state school either ... When we came back the two of us just wanted any kids we had to have a different experience – we felt separate schooling did damage, it was very limiting.'

Colm Murray-Cavanagh, involved from soon after ACT's foundation, says, 'I came back in one of the worst years, and I always had it in my mind that there were going to be an awful lot of pieces to be picked up in the end, got involved in community work in Derry and went to ACT meetings. The two of us were involved by then: Anne was preached against from the pulpit for being a Catholic teaching in a controlled school.'

The record shows an enterprise begun with considerable daring and selflessness, on the part of parents, teachers and supporters. Lagan opened in 1981 with two full-time teachers, four part-timers with a fifth appointed inside a fortnight, and twenty-eight pupils, in a scout hall on the fringes of affluent and then mainly Protestant south Belfast. It was one of the worst periods of the Troubles, a year marked by the controversy surrounding the deaths of ten republican prisoners on hunger strike. Many more people died violently, a total of 117 in the year, of whom republicans killed 64. The last hunger strike death came on 20 August.

Even a brief examination of the death toll during those days is a reminder of the unremitting brutality of the Troubles at their height. It also reveals the backdrop of murderous hatred to an experiment in practical reconciliation. As the new school struggled to establish a normal routine in the first two weeks of September, there were five killings: a young soldier, a Sikh from Birmingham, shot when he and a colleague were lured back to a flat by two women; two police constables aged nineteen and twenty, the younger on his first patrol, killed when an IRA landmine exploded under their car as they investigated a forest fire; a twenty-year-old full-time Ulster Defence Regiment (UDR) soldier shot on duty on a Saturday afternoon; and a young police reservist who visited his wife and their newborn baby in hospital and was then shot in the car park. A few hours earlier he had carried the coffin of the UDR man, a close friend. In the rest of the month six more people died, four more security force members and two Catholic civilians, one chosen at random by loyalists cruising a Catholic area looking for a victim, the other killed by the IRA because they said he gave information to the police.

The passions of the hunger strike left the two main communities looking at each other with sharpened and perhaps unprecedented mutual distaste, in some cases with open hatred. Many moderate Catholic nationalists as well as traditional republican supporters wholeheartedly backed the prisoners in their demands for 'political status', the right to be treated effectively as prisoners of war. When British Prime Minister Margaret Thatcher refused the hunger strikers' demands and they began to die, a huge swathe of Irish nationalism north and south of the border was tugged into sympathy, as an observer at the time put it, as though by a communal umbilical cord. Many, perhaps most, Protestants meanwhile watched the crowds at the funerals of the hunger strikers with indignant disbelief or angry revulsion. To them these were murderous terrorists, using a pacifist form of protest to gain unmerited sympathy and undermine law and order.

The atmosphere was stormy. Each prison death brought rioting and IRA revenge killings. In republican districts the walls read 'Break Thatcher's back'; in loyalist places there were equally vindictive black jokes about starving hunger strikers. Even to some of those disposed to be sympathetic, it seemed the least suitable moment to launch a school designed to teach children from the two sides in the same classroom, avowedly in an atmosphere of equal respect for Protestantism and Catholicism, and for both cultural traditions. To others, the very depth of polarisation made the

Lagan venture all the more right and remarkable. Stephen Pittam of the Joseph Rowntree Charitable Trust recalls one of the first approaches for financial help: 'We have no teachers and no building, they said, but we have more than twenty kids, and we're starting a school in four months – would you give us money for a head teacher? I remember the shivers up the back of my neck.' There was something daring above all, in his mind, in the willingness of parents to enrol children aged eleven in a nonexistent school: he was impressed at an educational enterprise built on what he saw as amazing faith and hope.

By contrast, many nationalists were disposed to see the Lagan effort as the latest in a long line of official attempts to deny that the Northern Ireland argument is primarily about political allegiance and to depict it instead as about 'sectarianism', defined as animosity between Protestants and Catholics, with both equally intransigent. Others were left cold by the location of the school, in Belfast's most affluent and at that point largely unmixed Malone Road, home of old Protestant money. The founders in fact had little choice, having searched elsewhere in vain over previous months. When it came to local realities, however, there was indeed an other-worldly, naïve quality to some of the pioneers. Brian Lambkin, the second teacher recruited, a Catholic brought up in England by Irish parents, remembers visiting the scout building which was to be the school's home for the first time, with the new principal, Sheila Greenfield, a brisk Englishwoman, and the second full-time teacher, Doreen Budd, a Presbyterian from County Down. 'There was a Union Jack covering one wall. I said we can't teach kids here, and Sheila and Doreen said, "Why not?" They genuinely saw nothing wrong with it.' He chuckled. 'Fortunately the people who ran the hall took the flag away so it wouldn't get chalky.'

Lagan's first principal had impressed the parents who interviewed her with her vivid personality, her experience of teaching in multifaith and multicultural English schools, and her strong commitment to the idea of comprehensive education – mixed-ability classes with a curriculum wider than the purely academic. The commitment to comprehensive education was a major point in Sheila Greenfield's favour: most of Lagan's first twenty-eight pupils had just been rejected in Northern Ireland's severe selective procedure for grammar school entry. It was another point that came to be used against the pioneers, that they wanted integrated education largely as a more socially desirable alternative to non-academic secondary schools. In conjunction with the impression that most of the movement's founders and many supporters were decidedly upper middle-class in their manner and background, the effect was to label the movement from the outset as 'do-gooding' and self-righteous.

Yet to people from other societies, it is nearly incomprehensible that, depending on the accident of birth, children slot immediately into one or other of Northern Ireland's two main communities and are schooled accordingly: the bulk of Catholics in the 'voluntary maintained' system, 'Catholic schools' in everyday speech, and most Protestants in 'controlled' schools, described by many unionists as a 'state' sector, which in practice is almost completely Protestant in management and staffing and overwhelmingly Protestant in enrolment and culture.

Outsiders often fail to appreciate the degree to which Northern Ireland society is segregated; this is unsurprising, since many of its inhabitants dislike admitting the fact or manage to convince themselves that it is a new phenomenon. That many are actually disapproving, even hostile to integrated education, is beyond the comprehension of those from elsewhere. When they are told that polls regularly show majority support in Northern Ireland for the principle of integration, the confusion is complete. To discover that in spite of poll findings 4½ per cent of children are in integrated schools adds the final touch to a bewildering picture. If so many people say they approve, why do more not send their children to such schools? Why would anyone be hostile to a simply expressed parental wish for children to be schooled together?

Even if all those who tell pollsters they support integration were sincere, and even if they meant they supported true integration rather than a dishonest substitute, neither of which is true, some would still be unable to enrol children because of the location of schools, and because many integrated schools cannot cope with demand. In the minds of the most frustrated supporters, it is an almost perfect vicious circle: more demand than supply and not enough demand to guarantee more supply, in part because insufficient supply depresses the confidence that would stimulate more demand. The development of further schools is a complex and disturbing consideration; there are various approaches, with disagreement about the best way forward between the authorities and some in the integrated sector.

The most fundamental question, as to why anyone would be less than supportive of schooling children together, is the most easily answered. Northern Ireland's schools are separate because of history and politics, and the two main communities remain divided in political culture: Catholics who are mainly nationalist and Irish in their political identity, Protestants who are chiefly unionist and British. The Good Friday Agreement's framework for power-sharing and parity of esteem pleases nationalists and has befuddled unionists. It is possible that more settled and mutually acceptable political arrangements will emerge, but equally possible that the fragile advance of consensus to date will stagger to a halt and even fall back. The peace process has immensely improved the atmosphere by reducing the number of deaths due to paramilitary violence, but has yet to broach significantly the agonising business of reconciliation. Segregation built on mutual mistrust, amounting in much of the population to hatred, avowed or not, is the product of centuries.

Separate schooling is matched by segregated housing, and despite more than two decades of legislation against discrimination in employment, a considerable number of people still work largely with others of their own religious background, or have workplace habits shaped by years of being in a tiny minority or a large majority. The result is caution, lack of openness, and unwillingness to raise any subject that might be thought contentious. Unsurprisingly, many go on to marry within the community into which they were born, and the cycle continues. Where to break it? Some do not in the least want to, and see no need for any significant change in the system. Many argue that segregated schooling has little bearing on the bitterness that sustained violence over the last third of the twentieth century. Others are convinced that separation throughout childhood, in a society that is otherwise highly segregated and divided politically, must be a major factor in maintaining, if not feeding, mistrust and hatred built largely on mutual ignorance.

'Voluntary segregation in housing, education, marriage – the institutions which help shape us and in which we live out most of our lives – is limiting, even destructive,' says Tom, a parent in a mixed marriage. 'Understandable, but destructive.' Jean, with a background in senior educational management, looks warily around at family and friends, most of them in relationships that do not move outside the communities they were born into, and makes a comment she admits she could not voice to siblings, parents, or many friends: 'The housing areas, schools and the marriages may often be excellent – but in our society maybe they all too often reinforce a wariness. There's suspicion of difference, rather than appreciation of, and respect for, diversity. That's almost an exotic idea in many minds.'

For many of those who send their children to the deliberately mixed schools established since 1981, there are few illusions, but some still cherish a sense of mission. A founder parent of an integrated primary says, 'I don't go with the injured innocence of Catholic and state schools when they protest that they too inculcate respect for other traditions. It's a bit like learning about elephants in class – you aren't actually going to see an elephant, but here's a photograph of one.' This parent was from a different background to the young mother who had never known 'a Taig', though also originally Protestant; his experience was suburban rather than inner-city, and he had spent time out of Northern Ireland. Like many younger parents who became involved in setting up integrated schools, he had less interest in the rift between Protestants and Catholics and the exploration of shared Christianity than the chief founders of Lagan, who regarded this as a central relationship to be tackled in integrated schools. 'What's missing because this place is so segregated is the constant low-intensity mixing that is the norm for schoolchildren elsewhere,' he said. 'That's what I wanted for our boys, not formal, self-conscious approaches to religious integration, none of that.'

The two parents whose children inspired the launch of Lagan and thus sparked the development of integrated schools in Northern Ireland could not have been more different from each other, or from many later founder parents. Tony Spencer was an impassioned English Catholic who taught sociology in Queen's University, with strong opinions about the reasons for the sectarian divide; Maeve Mulholland was a Protestant from County Down, a nursery teacher, a veteran of several peace movements, and an Alliance Party supporter. Like Spencer, she had joined ACT in 1974, when the Troubles were at their worst but with the first power-sharing experiment being put in place in Stormont.

She remembers well how the possibility of founding their own school first arose, as she stood beside Spencer at the back of an ACT fundraising function in early 1981. They had both been supporters for some time of ACT, an organisation set up initially by Catholic parents who sent their children to state schools because they disliked the separate Catholic system. As well as a shared belief that segregation had bad effects, and a desire to do something that would improve what they both saw as scandalously bad relationships between Christians, these two had a personal reason for wanting a new kind of school. 'We started chatting and he said, "I hear you have an eleven-year-old son. I have this eleven-year-old girl, Jane, and we need a school for her." I said gosh I could get really excited about that, because my husband and I didn't know where we were going to send Campbell.'

Another parent, who attended one of the earliest meetings to drum up support for the Lagan venture, vividly remembers Spencer's opening statement: 'I have a problem: her name is Jane.' As Mulholland says, 'The rush was on then. That was March/April. We had to have a school up and running by September. It would have been no good to us any later. It was very exciting, and nerve-racking too. Tony Spencer's never got his due really – I mean, I got an MBE and he got nothing. And it wouldn't have happened without him. I remember another meeting, when we wanted to appoint Sheila Greenfield. I heard Tony talking to his wife Rosemary and he was saying, "Could we take a second mortgage on our house?" The mortgage was to pay the salary of the principal: that's how dedicated the man was, and Rosemary too.' In the event, the Rowntree Trust came through with the money for salaries.

For Spencer, the Lagan venture was a crusade in which an interest he had pursued for some time took on an overlay of personal need. Without a new integrated school, Jane and Campbell were destined the following September for secondary schools, which then as now suffered from lack of status, were less popular with ambitious teachers than grammar schools, and in enrolment and staffing were in the vast majority of cases 100 per cent Catholic or Protestant. Many grammar schools have a particularly local prestige, but all are regarded as providers of essential grounding for employment in middle-class occupations. They provide the orthodox, if stuffy and conservative, form of academic teaching increasingly abandoned in England in favour of comprehensive, all-ability schooling. In both state and Catholic versions, examination success dominates the ethos.

Friends often ask if 'integrated' parents have thought through the implications of integrated education for their children, education-ally and socially as well as in terms of identity. Sometimes this questioning is overt and extremely hostile. Both Catholics and Protestants report bitter family arguments, with parents, and almost as often siblings, urging them to reconsider 'for the sake of the children'. A Catholic parent told academic researchers in 1992, 'Initially other members of the family were absolutely appalled. I have an uncle who is a parish priest and it went down like a bomb. Apart from the complexities of the situation from a religious point of view, people thought it was a very middle-class, trendy thing to do. They thought we were playing with our child's education.' A Protestant parent who met name-calling hostility to the idea of Protestant children being taught with Catholics said, 'The people here were ignorant, they didn't understand. They thought we were mad and a few didn't like it at all. They thought we were sending him with "Fenians", as they put it, to a Fenian school' (Alex McEwen and John Salters, *Integrated Parents: the Views of Parents*, Queen's University Belfast, 1992).

In the early meetings before setting up one primary school, a Protestant parent admitted, with visible difficulty, that she was having to negotiate every step of the way with her Protestant partner, who would allow their child to attend but did not want to be personally involved: 'It's as if he can handle the family and the mates as long as he isn't down there himself.' A Catholic in a rural area said he had yet to tell his elderly grandparents that their first grandchild would be going to the newly established local integrated school, rather than to the Catholic school he had himself attended: 'I'm trying to pick the best moment. They'll be destroyed – or they'll say they are. It'll be a child lost to the faith in their book, even though the school's working hard to find a properly qualified Catholic teacher to prepare the children for the sacraments. I can't imagine how I'd have told them if I was going to marry a Protestant.' Some years later, he said with some relief and still evident surprise that in fact his family had 'come round' to some degree. He thought the fact that the first Catholic teacher appointed came from another local family had made the difference, 'so we weren't the only ones doing this mad, odd thing'.

Parents suggest that family reaction to integrated primaries tends to focus around the obvious religious dimension involved, while integration at secondary level brings criticism, open or discreet, of the educational disadvantage children might suffer. Integrated schools are still new and relatively untried, many point out, unlike Northern Ireland's battery of proven grammar schools, tooled to produce the props and stays of what are effectively two establishments: the former unionist Protestant ruling class, and the nucleus of what is now a much-expanded Catholic bourgeoisie – lawyers, doctors, teachers and priests. What about the A levels, friends ask, the chance of getting into law, Oxbridge?

The grammar school sector in Northern Ireland has an unrivalled draw: it is available free to a middle class which sees many of their

counterparts in Britain paying through the nose for private schooling to avoid comprehensives. What selective education has meant
for the less favoured sector is not to be dwelled on: duty to your
own children first is the argument. There has been just enough
opportunity for working-class children to make it into grammar
schools to maintain an illusory sense of fairness and salve consciences. Transformation of the public face of Northern Ireland in
recent years from predominantly Protestant/unionist/British to
something that is increasingly Catholic/nationalist/Irish has on the
face of it reinforced rather than diminished separate schooling, in
that both sectors are now producing potential or actual movers
and shakers.

It is another strike against integrated schools that they are, or have
been, thoroughgoing comprehensive schools. A worry for a considerable number in the sector is that under parental pressure to
achieve higher academic grading, some of the schools are now
steering a path away from the comprehensive ideal. A considerable
section of this society across the sectarian divide is obsessed with
traditional academic performance and is big on competition. It
treats league tables (abolished – with wide support – by the first
Sinn Féin minister for education, Martin McGuinness) with
reverence, and which either scorns or is puzzled by the nonconformist.

Some of the big, long-established Protestant grammar schools,
the most socially elevated and proud of their own status, then as
now had a mix of religions and even nationalities in their intake,
including small numbers of Catholics. Some of them boasted,
though discreetly, that this was an unfussy form of integration. It
is a frequent argument made against a separate integrated sector by
Protestants, frequently by unionist politicians and less publicly but
stubbornly by some teachers, that state schools are open to all, and
are therefore technically or potentially integrated. Tony Spencer
had no illusions about the extent to which the presence of Catholic
minorities in largely Protestant schools contributed to real integration. His arguments drew on family experience, about which,
when necessary, he had a sociologist's professional detachment.

For some time he had a son at the overwhelmingly Protestant Methodist College, 'Methody', a voluntary grammar particularly proud of its mix of religions and cultures. In a television interview at the time, Spencer mentioned his own Catholicism. As he subsequently described on many occasions, using it as an example of how a tiny minority would always be assimilated rather than decently reflected, he arrived home to find his son in great distress. Having successfully pretended to be Protestant to his classmates, he had now been unmasked as a Catholic, and by his own father.

Anecdotal evidence from many individuals confirms that the pattern is common. 'I know a child who went through an integrated primary and is now at our big local grammar. Very proud that it has Catholics in it, though there's never been more than a handful. And he has yet to tell anyone in his class that he's Catholic,' said an integrated education supporter in a rural district. One parent became a tireless campaigner for integrated education having earlier enrolled children in the public school attended by their father. 'But we know they've been bullying Jim [not his real name] as "a Fenian" from the start. This is in one of the most upmarket schools in Northern Ireland! Endless cracks at him, in the showers, on the rugby field.' The parents tackled the subject with the school and were not satisfied with the response – that their son must toughen up. However, they decided it would be more disruptive to move him.

Six years after Lagan was established, Tony Spencer wrote in an academic work that in the first place, he was struck by the fact that 'unlike Protestants and Anglicans elsewhere in the English-speaking world, Protestants in Northern Ireland are most reluctant to send their children to schools under Catholic control, but expect Catholics to have their children educated at schools under Protestant control.' In the absence of proportionate numbers of Catholics among teachers and recognition by the schools of nationalist identity, Catholic children in de facto Protestant schools were in fact encouraged to 'keep a low profile'.

Spencer noted acidly that such schools, and the parents of the Protestant unionist majority in them, were 'encouraged to think that they are in the vanguard of the movement for better community relations via education. They tend to develop a complacency that obstructs ... strategies of co-operation and curricular development. And their satisfaction with this one-sided arrangement leads them to argue that the creation of planned integrated schools is unnecessary and "divisive".' It was not surprising, he added, that the nationalist community saw enrolment of Catholics in state schools as leading to assimilation, or even to proselytising.

For Maeve Mulholland, Spencer's fellow pioneer, the launching of a shared school was less a crusade than a logical follow-on from her earlier ventures – Women Together (a group set up in the early seventies when the Troubles' death toll was at its highest, to bring women together to 'work for peace'), the Peace People, and the Alliance party. She joined ACT with high hopes, much as she remembers believing that Women Together and in turn the peace movement in 1976 were bound to succeed because 'they brought people on to the streets demanding peace', because they showed that so many people clearly wanted the violence to stop. 'I was a joiner, I suppose. When I look back we were so optimistic, we just thought everybody was out marching, wanting peace, we were so young and naïve, so it would happen. We never envisaged it would take another thirty years to get agreement. You thought everybody wanted the same as you.'

She did notice, however, that only one of her friends chose to send a child to Lagan. 'People still say to me, "we would like to have done that but we didn't dare, you were very brave," as though we were going to be shot or something. They wouldn't have been willing to take that chance with their children's education. I suppose it was a risk. You were aware of it all right, that your child might pay the price if it didn't work, or they weren't happy. We said to Campbell from the start that he had to tell us at any stage if he wasn't happy. But he was very happy at Lagan. It was a happy school.'

ACT had tried other strategies before the question of founding a school came up. Their first effort came with the help of the

Unionist minister of education in the short-lived 1974 power-sharing administration, Basil McIvor, who drew up a plan for shared religious schools. Massive loyalist protest brought the executive down before the scheme could be implemented or widely discussed. McIvor went on to give decades to integrated education as a fundraiser and governor of Lagan College, becoming the first chairman of the governing board in 1981. With the help of the Alliance peer Henry Dunleath, ACT drafted a bill in 1977 to allow existing schools to convert themselves into shared schools but were disappointed to find that the measure was ineffective. Support from Alliance and a number of liberal unionists delighted ACT, but brought mixed reactions from those outside. The conjunction may have cost them as much in terms of credibility with Catholics as it brought in terms of Protestant support.

Cecil (Cecilia) Linehan is the woman who wrote the first letter to the newspapers which brought others into ACT. A Dubliner living in the polite small town of Holywood on the north Down coast, she was at one point an Alliance Party election candidate. In her mind, shared schooling and Alliance Party politics were attempts to deal with a political and social situation she found stifling. A devout Catholic, she sent her children to state schools so they would mix with Protestants.

One of the first people to answer her public appeal for support was another southerner living nearby, Betty Benton. Benton and Linehan in particular caught attention in the late seventies as they challenged the Catholic bishop of Down and Connor, Dr Philbin, about his refusal to allow children to be confirmed – even though they had been prepared for the sacrament – if they had not attended Catholic schools. Like Spencer and several others of the initial group, Benton and Linehan were commanding personalities and, as others have noted, outsiders, perhaps less disposed to be fatalistic than native inhabitants about the rigid separation between the communities. An English nun, Sister Anna, somewhat exotically for Belfast an Anglican, was another high-profile supporter and went on to become a tireless and successful fundraiser for the next three decades across Europe and America.

The two 'women who challenged the bishop' were much interviewed, appeared on television, and wrote letters to newspapers north and south explaining their case. Linehan had considerable flair for presentation, and went on to travel widely as fundraiser and lobbyist for the still-small integrated sector. From the outset ACT was keen to demonstrate to the existing education sectors, and perhaps in particular to the Catholic church, that they were not anti-Catholic or disposed to confrontation, and above all that they did not seek secular education. Some observers believed that the dominant ACT figures hoped a few big 'mixed' grammars would in time opt to transform into formally integrated schools. Most were not initially persuaded by Spencer that they must set up their own school. The disagreement caused considerable friction, but was temporarily resolved until the question of setting up further schools arose. Leading ACT figures became deeply involved in establishing Lagan and identified with it, but balked at the prospect of starting further schools.

Cecil Linehan's continued involvement is a link from the original ACT to the present-day Northern Ireland Council for Integrated Education (NICIE). Accustomed to hearing carping – after more than two decades of campaigning – that integration is 'only for the middle class', she moves smartly to the attack when the subject is raised. 'I asked a woman recently who said to me, "Pity they're not where they're needed," if she knew Malone.' Malone Integrated College is a secondary school on an increasingly tense borderline between Catholic and Protestant districts, where Catholics have moved into streets once entirely Protestant. The location is one that Maeve Mulholland says the Lagan pioneers would have loved, instead of the setting in the hills south-east of Belfast where the school eventually settled, to which some pupils travelled long distances. 'That actually is one of the things that always sticks in my mind,' Linehan says: 'the spread, from Antrim to the depths of Downpatrick. These kids were barely eleven as you know, and their parents were willing to let them travel those distances.'

The 'middle-class' tag stuck, did damage, and is much resented.

'We weren't all middle-class,' says Maeve Mulholland, 'and many weren't all that wealthy.' But a strong middle-class flavour may have been inevitable in a movement of parents to start new schools which implicitly challenged both existing sectors, which had to lobby government and business for support, and which had to find homes for their schools in mixed districts, almost inevitably of middle-class housing.

'Parent-driven', a senior inspector once called integrated education, though parent-led would be more accurate. The development originated entirely from the efforts of individuals, initially without any kind of official or organisational backing, and in the face of hostility and obstruction. At every point for many years, it is a story of stunning nerve by many people: parents, teachers and those who lent or granted them the money to sustain schools until government finally recognised their viability. It began with years of anxious effort to set up and establish Lagan, a pattern repeated with subsequent schools. Maeve Mulholland remembers the search for premises as particularly wearing, but also exciting: 'I remember Tony would ring and say he'd found this place, and we'd all dash off. There was a woman who supported us who had a lovely old house, we looked at that, all kinds of places: a disused arts centre outside Lisburn, and the building that eventually became Hazelwood Integrated College, over in north Belfast. But we wanted the south.'

Mulholland still has the class lists for the first five years of the school for driving the school minibus and other duties. They testify to how hands-on involvement was: children's names with names of parents and their telephone numbers underneath. At the end of the first term, as they grew out of the scout hall, there was another chase for classrooms. Sheila Greenfield and the other teachers took the entire enrolment away for hastily arranged field trips while alterations were made to a redundant special-school building. At one of their most desperate points they learned that a Catholic school had unused Portakabins, but the school refused to make them available, Mulholland still recalls with exasperation, 'Can you believe that? They didn't need them but we weren't going to get them.'

The effort to establish Lagan took time, effort and a degree of bloody-mindedness. Lambkin remembers that each successive year there was a problem about having mobile classrooms in place for the new intake in September. 'For the term beginning September 1983 we had to teach the first years in the old manor house at the Ulster Folk and Transport Museum in Cultra, in the County Down countryside.' To some, it felt as though Lagan had only just been established when Spencer proposed to start more schools in 1985. When Lagan won grant aid and maintained status in 1984, it was a watershed: battle commenced between the more or less exhausted consolidators, as one close observer ruefully recalls, and the expansionist Spencer. New schools would endanger Lagan, said most of ACT, to Spencer's impatient insistence that having set out on the path to provide an alternative, they had a moral duty to forge on when other parents wanted integration for their children. The disagreement caused much emotion. A much younger parent involved in opening two of the 1985 schools, but unaware until then of how the move had split ACT, recalls 'a meeting in the Quaker hall with Tony Spencer in the middle of the floor, chin set, and his wife bursting into tears, people taking her out – it was awful, actually'.

With a few others, Spencer formed a new group to support more schools, the Nuffield Foundation became a major financial supporter, and the drive continued, with emotions eventually cooling and some friendships mended in time. 'We left bodies behind us, no doubt,' a founding figure ruefully reflects. Another remembers being told by a charitable trust official, encountered at a particularly turbulent moment, that no significant and long-lasting enterprise built on voluntary effort escaped acrimony: 'This was no good to me at all.'

The storms were a foretaste of strains down the years in several schools, but in the end did not deter the next step – the foundation on the same day in autumn 1985 of three schools, a primary and secondary both called Hazelwood in north Belfast, and a second primary, Forge, in south Belfast. Some of those involved were taken aback to find that establishing schools to bring children together should involve strong, sometimes ferocious disagreement.

Some were relieved to find that the battles had nothing to do with religious or political difference. For others, it seemed entirely predictable and not at all worrying that pioneers should be 'toughies who liked a scrap', as one says now with a smile. 'We've definitely got our share of pushy parents,' one of the early head-teachers said more than ten years into the story, in an off-the-record conversation with a group of reporters. 'But then without pushy parents would there have been any integrated schools?'

One parent, an educationalist by occupation, says resignedly of arguments witnessed about management and practice in various schools over the years, 'It's the price you pay for believing in parents, and parent-power, and people-power. Perhaps to some degree the trouble was born out of naïvety. But then if you were cool and sophisticated would you be in this?' An afterthought offers a sense of perspective with which many who are equally experienced agree: 'And there are probably a lot more teachers and parents who have come through unscathed or think what happened has been mainly to their advantage.'

A more abrasive assessment voiced often though not in public by people involved in various capacities, is that among parents and perhaps also teachers, the integrated sector clearly attracts a quota of the difficult, some bordering on the obsessional. 'Like all schools,' says a veteran teacher who supports integration. 'You get difficult parents everywhere. It's just that these are schools founded by parents, and for some that's an invitation to put their pet theories into action. Not all of which are entirely sane,' she adds, 'and occasionally you find they've tried them on the two older sectors first.'

Hazelwood was very different from the Lagan flagship from the outset and has remained so, a gritty school in a tough spot where a growing number of working-class Catholics live close to working-class Protestants who increasingly complain that north Belfast has 'gone green'. Not all integrated schools represent such a spread, a longtime supporter involved in various ways admits carefully. 'That's what pleased me so much about Hazelwood. To the argu-ment that pushing for integrations is preaching to the converted, well, look at the place. Hazelwood is a mixture not just of religion but of class too.'

Like Forge Primary, opened on the same day and similarly mixed socially, Hazelwood also represented a new breed of parent in the tiny integrated world. A considerable number in Hazelwood and in Forge wanted to be closely involved in every aspect of setting up the new schools, from choosing staff to deciding the contents of the curriculum, and school policy on homework, uniform, competition, how sexism should be defined and countered, and how comparative religion should be taught – or not. A sizeable number originally volunteered to take after-school 'clubs' in subjects that were difficult or impossible to timetable, largely because small new staffs at first contained no one qualified to teach them: languages, including Irish, music and art were the most common and most warmly welcomed by teachers. Some Spencer associates called this wish for hands-on and detailed contribution 'deep parental involvement'. Others listened with wariness, even bafflement.

Some of those early parents remember the period as golden: 'I remember teams of parents, very mixed in every way, getting Forge ready,' says one. 'Fixing broken windows, cleaning toilets and classrooms.' A Belfast woman from a working-class background, Shona, says, 'It was the most creative I've ever felt.' She offered one of the new schools an after-school art club and also volunteered as a reading assistant. 'If you grew up thinking of teachers as these bossy, overbearing creatures who couldn't be challenged, all of them so middle-class, it was a way to make sure that didn't happen again to your child. Nobody was going to behave like that if you were coming in to the school every day, or that's what I thought.'

Shona is unusually frank; many other believers in deep parental involvement admitted their motivating dread of arrogant teachers only after clashes began, which did not take long. Probably the most angry and divisive were about the wish some had to shape school policy: it was the area teachers objected to most openly, and about which a considerable number of principals in particular are still concerned.

Some parents were happy to leave school policy to the principal, after initial meetings and discussion. These were people who had modest wishes. Having set up schools 'with our bare hands', as one says now, 'all I wanted was to be sure that they didn't turn into the sort of place that has a sign up inside the front door: "No parents beyond this point." ' A sign with precisely that message hung in Malone Primary School – whose building later became that of Forge – according to the veteran lobbyist Anne Odling-Smee: it was where her children went before the integrated movement began.

To a number of parents who wanted integrated schools to be different but had no personal ambitions to be involved at such a level, 'deep parental involvement' quite rapidly became bad news. 'It was code for interference in a big way,' says one who took children out of the sector within years. 'There were some parents there you could never have satisfied, and the teachers' backs just went up immediately. It was a bad atmosphere.' He remembers several couples who were insistent that their school must have no Irish, because as Catholics they felt Irish had 'ghettoised' them, and who also wanted to be given a school policy on sexism in the first weeks of the first term, so they could be sure 'feminism' had not found its way into the ethos.

Another remembers considerable acrimony because some teachers had talked about 'God' in front of the whole class, not just the Catholic children preparing for communion and confession – although it had been clearly stated in advance that the school would do this, and that it recognised the centrality of Christianity in Northern Ireland society. These were parents who also demanded that Irish be taught to all, and that the school sign up to a thorough-going policy 'to combat sexism', as a bruised member of the first board of governors remembers: 'Basically they wanted us to make sure their little girl never heard about religion, learned to speak Irish, and started playing with spanners instead of dolls. They wanted the lot.'

In this later wave of parents, the wish to play down the Christian ethos of integration was more widely shared, however, than by a few parents passionate across a range of demands. Lagan's original parents had all appeared to share with Tony Spencer and Maeve Mulholland a commitment to the centrality of Christianity in education, or at least none publicly disagreed. Several of the younger generation, however, and many more since to judge by a random sample encountered while writing this book, have been much keener on being recognised, and having their children recognised, as neither Catholic or Protestant but 'other', or 'none', than they were on formally trying to integrate children of the two Christian denominations.

Michael, a parent with one child just through a secondary integrated college outside Belfast and another about to leave the local integrated primary, says, 'I felt it was the only way that my child, who has no religion, would be able to go in as a fully-paid up member. I didn't want them going in as also-rans,' he says. 'That was my own baggage – as a kid in different types of school I was excused from religion or the only one who refused to join in. If you have no religion in small communities in Northern Ireland you don't fit. You're a bit of a freak.' Jenny, whose children go to Lagan, is not as concerned that her children's 'otherness' should be recognised and accepts that integration of Protestants and Catholics is the main aim of the sector. But she finds what she calls 'Lagan's relentless religiosity' a bit hard to take. 'My boy is a first year and he seems to spend his entire time in what I thought would be a comparative religion class talking about local churches. They visit them, and they draw them, and they write about them, and then they build them. I have a church that he made in the boot of the car at the minute.'

Jenny is rueful about the church-building, however, and amused rather than seriously disturbed. She thinks she might feel different if she lived somewhere else. She is less concerned than Michael in deepest mid-Ulster about her girl and boy feeling different, because they live in reasonably mixed south Belfast. They also have a wider family and circle of friends which is laid-back and of several religious backgrounds, with many friends of several races in England, where both children were born. Her children know others who are 'other', and always have; they have no concept that some regard two forms of belief as constituting a norm from which everyone else deviates.

Michael, in a small, chiefly Catholic town where everyone knows everyone else's business, needed more reassurance, perhaps more camouflage, for his unbaptised, religion-blind child. 'The primary's been grand,' he says now. 'They do the confession and communion bit discreetly and I like the fact that they all celebrate the big day for the wee Catholic kids. But the secondary's getting a bit iffy. Protestants have been leaving because where the school is has steadily become more Catholic. So the mix isn't so hot anymore.' What happens next, says a seasoned supporter, 'is the Protestant parents lose confidence and go'.

In contrast with those who are uneasy at the religious element, many parents have chosen integrated education with little personal interest in religion. But they do have a wholehearted conviction that an emphasis on what Protestants and Catholics share, and a commitment to explain one denomination to the other, is vital to what they think the sector should be doing. For Tom, the parent in a mixed marriage who thought segregated living was 'limiting, even destructive', the way his boys were presented in Forge and in Lagan with a positive image of the sacraments of confession and communion, and with the custom of Ash Wednesday, was valuable, even heart-warming. 'I loved that. I loved the way the kids came back all pleased for their friends who got a big day out, the party they had in class afterwards – to make up, though they didn't know it, for some priest's hard-heartedness in keeping them away from their own parish's communion day. The school did that very well. Balloons and cake: that took any menace suspicious Protestants could have sniffed out of the day.'

He was equally impressed with Lagan's Ash Wednesday custom of gathering the school together to see Catholic pupils, and teachers, receive 'that black smudge on their foreheads. When I think what that meant as I was growing up – an odd, slightly spooky thing on the few Catholics who lived round us.' Jean, also from a Protestant background and with experience in educational management at a senior level, makes a similar observation but adds to it, 'That's so important, because I know how you couldn't do it in any state school without uproar from any number of parents – doesn't matter what schools with some degree of mix tell you about their wonderful relations. They none of them, to my knowledge, do what Lagan does. And it's so valuable. You're talking about voodoo here to some people. That's what integration should be about, taking the nightmares out of unfamiliar religious practices.'

In parts of Belfast, and elsewhere in Northern Ireland, some choose integrated education almost as much, it seems, to find schooling that will involve a social mix as well as a mix of religions. Some would prefer no emphasis on religion, and want to be sure that their child is not in a largely middle-class environment, either as a political principle or simply because they do not regard themselves as middle class and want their children to have a sizeable number of schoolmates from a similar background.

To judge from conversations specifically for this book but also over years with parents in integrated schools across Northern Ireland, many are happy with the class mix of their children's school. Some, however, are uneasily aware that parents among them have chosen integration for social reasons, as the more socially desirable option in nongrammar secondary education. Others think from observation of school practice that their schools might have chosen the line of least resistance on the touchiest issues of communal identity. The issues of class and identity converge in a place that has seen a number of the most significant clashes and political developments in the course of the last four decades.

In the north's second city, which unionists insist must be called Londonderry, while nationalists are as determined to call it Derry, the founders of integrated schools agonised and came up with the device of Derry/Londonderry, or for preference 'L'Derry', (pronounced 'El Derry'), on headed notepaper and in discussions. It is not a compromise that endears them to a considerable number of the city's population who live on the west bank of the river Foyle, an area almost completely Catholic and in part strongly republican, many very conscious of being working class and living in some of the most deprived estates in Northern Ireland. Joanne, adamant that she and her partner are 'nonsectarian' rather than Catholic or Protestant, said that she could see the need for sensitivity and accepted the usage Derry/Londonderry in her mixed Protestant/ Catholic workplace. 'El Derry' made her scoff, but as a west bank dweller she had other reasons for choosing what was originally an almost totally Protestant primary school.

The Model School was close at hand and had changed character – from the beginning of the Troubles, Protestants had left for the other side of the river, the Waterside. Joanne found the school attractive chiefly because it was secular, she said. 'It's the real thing, not the fraud that unionists pass off as integrated: it's a proper state school with no religion in it but a real mix of religion. Because it's on the edge of the Bogside it has a social mix as well. There are children there whose parents are from some of the poorest estates in Derry. And I think nearly every child of mixed race in Derry goes there, it's become a tradition.'

This might be slightly exaggerated. A second west bank resident, a single parent, chose the Model as a primary but sends his secondary-age mixed-race child to Oakgrove. 'They've done very well by Sheila and I'm really pleased. It seems to me they're kind, and they work at the inclusive thing, which I was worried about in advance. What I heard was that if you were a working-class kid you might feel out of it, but that's not true for my daughter.' Like the other west banker, Fergus and his child are neither Protestant nor Catholic but wholehearted atheists, 'others' in the original termin-ology of integrated education. Clearly he felt that this proved no drawback in Oakgrove.

A few analysts have begun to note the numbers of Catholics in state schools and think they detect a significant rise. A total of 6,965 in the year 2000/2001 was logged by the Department of Education for Northern Ireland (DENI), the largest component of which, by a considerable distance, was the number at state or controlled primaries – 3,229. The custom of largely middle-class Catholics sending children to the biggest and best-known Protestant gram-mars is long-established. Enrolment at primary schools is a new phenomenon to some. Catholic children at state nurseries number 1,292, according to the figures, but nursery provision until very recently was scarce in Catholic primary schools. On examination, it also emerges that some of the schools involved, like the Model and increasingly Foyle Grammar (also on Derry's west bank), have become 'mixed' as Protestants leave districts: Vere Foster primary school in west Belfast and Tullygally in Craigavon, County Armagh, are both recognised as having altered largely as a result of changes in their catchment areas. Catholics, it seems, are not surprisingly more disposed to send their children as state schools become less Protestant. 'But it's gone too far now,' Joanne laments. 'The Model's becoming predominantly Catholic, it's had a Catholic principal for years and I think many of the teachers are Catholic now too.'

The other surprise for some in the DENI figures is the sizeable number registered as 'no religion, not recorded', a total of more than 17,000. The debate on the demographic balance has sharpened, with expectations that work on the recent census will show that the margin of Protestant majority has already diminished to no more than a few percentage points. Already, the identity of DENI's non-religious, 'other' children has become a factor in the argument that springs up each time new census figures are imminent. Those who dislike speculation about disappearance of the long-lasting Protestant majority in Northern Ireland are inclined to suggest that the bulk of these 'other' children are in fact Protestant. Others wonder, perhaps more reasonably, if they might not in fact be what the figures suggest – unaffiliated to any denomination.

Some wonder if the combination of what is probably a growing trend of mixed Protestant/Catholic marriage and the growth of integrated schooling has already begun to produce a generation that is genuinely neither Catholic or Protestant, neither British or Irish, but 'mixed', like the parents to whom they were born and who sought integrated schooling for them. The proportion of mixed marriages among integrated school parents is variously estimated at 10 and 25 per cent (these two figures were cited within a year of each other, by a serious education specialist in the *Times* in 1991, and in the research by Queen's University Belfast academics Alex McEwen and John Salters in 1992). A number of 'integrated' parents believe, from observation and experience, that the proportion is much higher than one quarter of all enrolment.

A well-disposed Dubliner once remarked that it was his experience of visits to Lagan and conversation with staff there in the early days that 'they became somewhat tense when you asked about balance of pupils, and indeed staff, how it was achieved. It seemed to me they particularly didn't like it when you asked what they did about people who are neither one nor the other.' The answer, according to many parents, is that schools put pressure on non-religious parents, especially those who are of mixed religious background, to say what their origins are and then to persuade them to allow their children to be registered in whichever column the school enrolment lacks. 'It makes my blood boil,' said one founder parent, 'but the Department puts them up to it.' The category 'both' does not exist for DENI.

Mixed marriage is in some minds the buried razor which cuts to the surface in most critical conversation about the subject. The fact that it is a phenomenon with a name is itself a comment on a society separated along basic fault lines, which can and do regularly erupt into danger and violence. Brian Lambkin, one of Lagan's founder teachers and later its principal, wrote in the middle nineties, in the study that earned him a doctorate, that 'the fundamental objection to integrated education is that it may lead to mixed marriage'. Lambkin had been quoting the archbishop who headed the Church of Ireland in 1943, J.A.F. Gregg, on the subject of the Catholic Church decree enforced in Ireland from 1908, 'Ne Temere', which insisted that the children of all mixed marriages must be brought up Catholic. Many southern Protestants and even more in Northern Ireland blame 'Ne Temere', still in operation until the early 1970s, for the dwindling Protestant population in the Republic. Gregg urged Protestants not to:

… throw their children into unnecessary association with Roman Catholics. If the barrier is broken down or even weakened, those who played together as children will naturally say when they grow up: 'If you let us play together then, why should we not marry now?' Keep up the distinction, I would entreat you.

Not all parents in mixed marriages send their children to integrated schools. Some clearly choose a school with whose ethos one partner is more identified than the other, and for others integrated schools do not smooth away all the difficulties. 'You only want an integrated school because you're mixed': this assertion is often delivered as though it were an accusation, somehow implying bad motivation. Several predominantly youthful parents at one of Belfast's integrated primaries braved the subject in a parent–teacher association meeting in 2001. 'I want my child's questions about sectarian clashes answered in school,' said a young mother who introduced herself as being in a mixed marriage, 'because it causes trouble enough at home when we talk about confession and communion.' The subsequent conversation touched on the then controversial and bitterly divisive loyalist attacks on small schoolgirls and parents walking to the Catholic Holy Cross primary in north Belfast's Protestant Glenbryn estate. There was a brief but relatively probing discussion about how the Holy Cross situation should be tackled in their children's classes, but no one took up the issue, clearly thornier, of how even in a mixed marriage an integrated school's treatment of religious practice could be touchy. Two observers sitting in on the meeting were struck by a shared determination to keep discussion light and to move sharply on when it threatened to become serious.

For many, the issue simply does not arise. No matter what the Catholic educationalist might assert, if the local Catholic or state school has a reputation as a good school academically, a pleasant place to learn, and is the neighbourhood favourite, only parents with a personal interest in integration go looking for an alternative. Separation is the norm and most people want to be part of the norm, without ever thinking twice about it. When they do think about it, many have such instinctive attachment to communal practice that they probably never seriously consider an alternative as a real proposition. Those who do are still the exceptions, and are very often looked at as having exceptional, and not always sympathetic, reasons for their individualistic choice.

'Are you being fair to them?' a mother was asked very seriously when the first integrated primary schools had just begun, with what seemed more genuine concern than desire to score points. 'Are you not afraid you might be doing this for your own reasons rather than for your daughter?' It is, of course, the question most likely to give pause to any parent with what others think is a bee in the bonnet about education, medical treatment, choice of diet, and lifestyle generally. An equally common reaction is to ask how the schooling of the parents had fallen short: 'Didn't the nuns do all right by you? Catholic education got the likes of you where you are today and now you turn your back on it.' The comment is usually made in light-hearted, joky fashion, but these are serious middle-class considerations.

While much political argument has taken place at high-decibel level, drowned out for many years by gunfire and explosions, the sound of silence also marks the most difficult subjects. Political figures have conducted a mostly sterile argument, in that they rarely if ever engage with each other; arguments tend to be a matter of starting from opposite premises and shouting past each other, or delivering lectures in tones unlikely to encourage a warm or respectful hearing. Integrated education is one area where some people have found a way to express a civic spirit, respect for others of different backgrounds and with different political identities. 'It's about finding a way of not feeling disenfranchised, that's why I got involved,' says Jan O'Neill, one of the founders of North Coast Integrated College, established in 1996, who supports integrated education by lobbying and fundraising. 'That was it for me too,' says Anne Odling-Smee, an early member of ACT, a firm believer in Tony Spencer's vision, and chair of the Integrated Education Fund (IEF) from 1995 for five years. 'It's community action,' she adds.

It is neither a simple nor an unthinking business, to be a parent of a child at an integrated school, even for some of those who spend least time on the decision or make it for the least idealistic reason – that an integrated secondary school is a more socially desirable option than the local state or Catholic secondary. In some minds, this might be a very large proportion of integrated secondary parents. Once assured of anonymity many teachers, parents and other pupils are frank: 'Seems to me many of my friends are in Lagan because they couldn't get into Methody or Rathmore,' a Belfast university student and former Lagan pupil said in 2001. 'It's certainly not because their parents believed in integrated education.'

It is a familiar pattern in Belfast and Derry, many say, as in other parts of Northern Ireland, though perhaps slightly less so where the local integrated college has only recently been established. One child or children in the family will be sent to prestigious grammars like Catholic Rathmore or increasingly mixed Methody, Belfast Royal Academy, and Victoria College in Belfast, or the well-known Derry convent school of Thornhill; a sister or brother will go to Lagan or Hazelwood, or to L'Derry's Oakgrove Integrated College. The more academic sibling goes to grammar school, the less academic to an integrated school.

The messages this frequent family practice sends to the children in each case hardly bear consideration, and the former Lagan pupil's knowing comment is difficult to dispute. It remains true that having sent a child off to mix in school, perhaps with no interest or taste themselves for meeting anyone outside their own community, parents are then faced with their daughter or son mixing out of school, bringing friends home, going to stay in a friend's house overnight, are faced too with meeting parents of the other community at the school gates. In a segregated society, this is often more association with the 'other side' than many are ever likely to have otherwise: integration by default perhaps, but integration to some degree none the less. As Jan O'Neill says cheerfully, 'A lot of people go into integration and the concept grows on them.' She thinks this is great – the unconverted reached, then in time converted.

The bulk of parents who choose integrated education are not activists of any kind, this much both experience and research suggest. They might be grateful that someone has cared enough to start and maintain a sector that gives them a choice other than segregation. Many talk warmly about integrated schooling as the ideal they always hoped to find, but they are not going to be involved at parent–teacher groups, in fundraising, or in political lobbying. They have tiring and busy lives, they want their child or children to be happy and well-taught, and they want not to think too much more about the whole business. For these parents, as for most, school is meant, certainly, to be a good and useful component of bringing up their children, but not to be a major part of their own adult lives. Leave the children there in the morning, pick them up after school or let them walk home, contribute financially if it is possible when the school asks for help, turn up to see a teacher if something is wrong or perhaps for parents' nights, and try to be there for the Christmas concert and the sports day: that would be an approximation of many attitudes.

Other than that, school is not meant to be labour-intensive or a focus of interest in the minds of most parents, and they try to keep it that way. They might admire individual teachers inordinately or have reservations. Either way, most do not want to do any part of the teacher's job. Some might have considerable personal commitment to the idea of integration. For these parents schooling might be an important part of their own self-image, and the fact of their choice is near the surface of their consciousness of who they are. Others want integration for their children but not, particularly, for themselves. A considerable number will have chosen integrated schools because they disliked the nearest school, or the school to which their child was allocated by the selection procedure. Their choice is made for educational, at least as often as for social reasons: perhaps a mixture of the two.

Once the moment of decision is past, most 'integrated' parents are not all that different from parents who send their children to the other sectors. The decision to send a child to an integrated school, however, is still a considerable move, a deliberate and conscious choice, which makes it just that bit different. For the overwhelming majority of all parents, picking a primary school tends not to be a major task – unlike the choice of a secondary school, which might involve a much wider family research exercise and considerable investigation, often involving the child in visits to several open days. Deciding to go for an integrated school, at either level, even for the least thoughtful parent, requires at the very least a decision against one or other of the two big sectors. A 'leap of faith', is how one parent from a strong Catholic background once described it.

Those who send their children to integrated schools are a mixture, like parents of children at any school, with the distinction that they attract opposition within their families and in social settings – and a degree of frank hostility – that is probably not the lot of parents who choose Irish-language schools, or the small number of independent Christian fundamentalist schools. Commitment to the Irish language, or to biblical Christianity, might be anathema to many, but in the wider communities relevant to both, it would not seem decent or respectful openly to criticise parents who make such a choice.

In an atmosphere where all consideration of identity is highly charged, the relatively simple desire that children should grow up alongside peers of other denominations, religions and no religion is rarely taken at face value. Challenge separate schooling, and you challenge separate identities and all that underpinned the old certainties: the charge is rarely so clearly put, but it lurks beneath much of the covert and overt distaste for integration.

One father of children who have attended both primary and secondary integrated schools becomes impassioned when asked what his reason was for choosing the sector. He did not have an elaborate philosophy to which schools and teachers must sign up. But distaste for their own experience of segregated schooling is for some a matter of principle; they refuse to inflict on their children the separation from contemporaries that was their own experience during their most formative years. This man's partnership, again, is mixed. But he echoes many in relationships with no religious or political mix when he eloquently describes the basic and unmatchable experience he thought integrated schools in Northern Ireland could deliver, provided only, as he stipulates, that they had a genuinely balanced intake of pupils, in a properly maintained atmosphere of mutual respect:

Sharing the experience of growing up can't but be valuable. It won't work sudden miracles and it often won't work at all – the children in integrated schools will still spend more time being influenced by family, street, churches. Copying each other's homeworks; smoking behind the bike sheds; lending sneakers to the friend who needs them for PE fourth period; going into town after school to buy tickets in Virgin for a concert; going to the concert; gossiping about teachers; bantering with each other about football teams or boyfriends/girlfriends; Valentine cards, Christmas cards; sleepovers; visiting each other's homes; helping friends through difficult patches in school or at home: the small change – but vital small change – of learning to relate to other people. That's what I wanted from integration, and that's what our boys got. And in Northern Ireland, it was only going to happen in a natural, nontokenistic way in an integrated school.

2
Friends

As north Belfast settled in 2001 into repeated sectarian clashes, a fundraiser for integrated education commented unguardedly, 'Things are depressing, aren't they. But people are more interested when things go badly, which is good for us in marketing. Not that it's what we want, of course ...' His voice tailed away, as he realised what he had just said.

Though it sounds bad when put so baldly, the connection is undeniable. At some of the most dispiriting periods of conflict, donations and offers of help for the project of integrated education have flooded in. In contrast, the comparative tranquillity at other points over the past few years, and previously, has on occasions made it difficult to arouse interest. On the other hand, it could be argued that the number of integrated schools has had its most rapid period of growth since the ceasefires of 1994, increasing from twenty-four to forty-seven. Of this list of 'new' schools, twelve were planned as integrated schools and started from scratch, and ten are formerly controlled schools that have chosen to 'transform'.

Some of those involved in integrated schools as teachers or parent-governors say their enrolment has gone up after a particularly awful atrocity: certainly fundraising has been easier. When times are hardest and violence seems unstoppable or once more on the rise, or when sectarian clashes recur with some new and savage twist, the cause of integrating the education of Northern Ireland's children suddenly seems most attractive again at home and elsewhere. The connection is that the subject, in many minds, cuts to the heart of the conflict.

Integrated education has many friends, many of whom have stuck with the cause for most of the past twenty years. 'Marketing' has begun to stage increasingly slick public occasions, involving friends like television star Joanna Lumley and former Northern Ireland Secretary Mo Mowlam, both of whom turned up at a NICIE awards ceremony in 2002 to compere, and make and receive presentations, with Mowlam promising to continue to support integrated education in any way she could. But the integrated education sector is still in the position of needing steady and sizeable donations, and has always found it more difficult to fundraise inside Northern Ireland. The features that attract foreign support might be precisely those that alienate closer to home. After decades of conflict and peace groups of varying effectiveness, there is considerable local resistance to 'hands across the barricades' rhetoric, in part because it has often come across as pious, sentimental, and overblown. In a bruised and disillusioned society, acclaim abroad from the uninformed has a sad habit of turning into mockery at home.

Support and friendship from one influential quarter, however, has always been a straightforward blessing. From the earliest stages, when the sector consisted of little more than a score of enthusiasts and about the same number of children, and even earlier when the idea was little more than an idea, a number of major British charitable trusts gave advice, encouragement and, within a short period, large sums of money in either grants or loans. Parents were the spur, the motive force, the drivers of the project, a constantly refilled reservoir of highly motivated volunteers – an unparalleled resource for any undertaking, as trust officials point out insistently. Many of those involved at the outset equally recognise that trust directors and officials were a propulsive outside force. Without them, it is hard to see how more than one school would ever have been established: Lagan would have been a lone standard-bearer, an experiment.

TRUSTS

The most significant contribution over an extended period was that of Anthony Tomei, now director of the Nuffield Foundation but in 1985 a youthful assistant director who delivered a sizeable Nuffield grant to an untested group with a vague project. It was a huge gesture of faith and confidence which lifted dreams into the realms of practicality and gave hope, meaning and purpose to further effort. 'I asked trustees to put up a quarter of a million pounds a year for three years,' he recalls. 'Quite a lot. And they didn't hesitate. They were so sure it was right. One trustee said, "This may well not work and it may turn out not to go the way we would like it to, but we must always remember that at the time we were making the right decision – the right thing to do at the right time."' This judgement, says Tomei, often came into his mind when he reflected on decision making. More than a decade later, he chooses to emphasise first what the resolution to support integrated education meant for charitable trusts, in terms of decision making and the course of their history in Northern Ireland:

> Apart from its intrinsic importance, for me it's one of the best examples of how an independent source of funding can really make a difference, in a situation where the politics have for all sorts of reasons precluded government from doing what it might otherwise have done. It's a terribly interesting case history from the funders' and the political point of view.

He also jokes that when first asked, he decided against giving money to integrated education, and that credit for the initial daring decision must go to Stephen Pittam of the Joseph Rowntree

Charitable Trust, the most knowledgeable and subtle of trust operators over the entire duration of the Troubles, like Tomei then more junior and now in charge of his trust's direction. The first approach for trust help on behalf of Lagan, only a few months before the school opened, seemed rash to Tomei, as indeed it did to Pittam. But Pittam recalls the 'shiver up the back of his neck'; he was drawn by the daring, and found the money to pay the principal's salary. An original Lagan parent remembers that 'some of those chocolate people gave us the money'. The two trust directors have a friendly running joke about Rowntree's leap in the dark, followed by Nuffield's much grander funding.

Though their generosity made a crucial difference, the trusts were crucial in other ways. They brought an invaluable extra dimension to integrated education: because big benefactors had taken it seriously, government took it seriously. 'The Department of Education line was basically, "Well, it'll never work",' one official remembers. The trusts set about exploring the possibilities of cooperation with government. 'The line basically was, "We can't stop it if parents want to do it but it's nothing much to do with us. Frankly, if you want to waste your time, that's fine." That's perhaps a slight caricature, but really what you got was benign scepticism.'

In time, indeed quite swiftly, the education authorities became involved to the extent that they began to have meetings with trusts, occasionally accompanied by campaigners for integration. The make-up of delegations mattered: trusts have varying approaches, but Nuffield knowingly uses its 'great and good' element of big names from the worlds of politics, academia and business to open doors and ensure a respectful hearing. ACT had always been convinced that they got a hearing in Stormont because former minister Basil McIvor led their delegations; some believed this played a major part in helping to win official recognition of Lagan inside three years. The trusts arrived from England with another layer of influence.

It worked for integrated education but it was also a style that fed suspicion among existing schools and gave ammunition to the wary and ill-disposed – that this was an infant sector given special treatment for political reasons, and that it lobbied through people with 'posh accents'. To those disturbed at the prospect of government officials beginning to move because they were impressed by the names or social status of lobbyists, it could of course have been argued that all lobbying is a matter of converting influence into pressure, and that the controlled, voluntary and maintained schools had been using their own influence astutely for decades past. But the 'middle-class' tag stuck, and did damage. So did the suggestion that the new schools were a form of social or political engineering, geared to depict the Northern Ireland quarrel as primarily one of sectarian enmity, which could be tackled without difficult accommodation of competing political identities.

At Nuffield, Rowntree, and the string of other foundations who made grants to integrated education on a smaller scale, though in some cases over lengthy periods to support individual schools or particular projects, the officials most involved were convinced about the merits of the case. It is clear they saw the schools primarily as a mechanism to bring the communities together. Accounts of the time from participants suggest there was little if any agonising in the Northern Ireland Office (NIO) about political intentions. Some in the trusts will also admit that although they wanted to see government funding for the new schools from the outset, since an unfulfilled parental demand clearly existed, they could see from an early stage that integration was indeed getting special consideration. 'It has to be said the rest of education was not that well funded across the board,' one recalls.

When government eventually shifted policy, in 1989, to fund new integrated schools from the outset, the trusts saw it as a vindication. 'It was a huge success in our terms,' says Tomei. 'We achieved what we wanted to achieve, which was to find ways of government funding these schools from the beginning.' For him, the striking qualities of those involved in setting up the early schools were courage and ambition as well as commitment, which he describes as 'their adventurous spirit, and willingness to take huge risks. In the early years there was a real sense of partnership between those involved in starting the movement, and the trusts supporting them.'

The few who dared to start Lagan, and those who then launched out into the venture of three more schools only four years later, were hugely buoyed by the warmth from charitable trusts and the personal kindliness of those they dealt with, almost as much as they were lifted by the awareness that this support meant large sums of money committed to making the schools happen. It is not easy to recapture now how vital such encouragement must have been to people starting out on a venture many deemed ill-advised and impossible.

Stephen Pittam, with more than thirty years experience of Northern Ireland, emphasises what the trusts gained from the experience: discovery of a way to work with government, and a lasting, comparatively uncontentious contribution. 'It's the traditional role of trusts to support innovative ideas which if successful would be picked up by government. This rarely happens now – but it did in this case.' Pittam makes little of the fact that people met warmth where they expected officialese, friendship and welcome where they were braced to withstand tough and unsympathetic questioning, but it is what many still remember most vividly from those early days.

The first approach came in a handwritten note to the Joseph Rowntree Charitable Trust in March 1981 from ACT, telling them that a consultation was about to begin over a fortnight on the idea of setting up an integrated school. The Rowntree records show that on 9 April ACT wrote to say that fifteen children were signed up for the school. In June the trust agreed a grant of £15,000 to cover a principal's salary and some running costs: in September, Lagan opened.

There was a history. Before the Lagan venture began, trusts financially supported the initially all-Catholic ACT to run classes to prepare their children, enrolled in controlled schools, for First Communion and confession. People knew that financial help was possible, and who to approach. It is argued against integrated education that middle-class involvement brought them support from an early stage that would not have been available to less wealthy or assertive groups. But charitable trusts have supported causes in Northern Ireland that include education schemes for paramilitary and ex-paramilitary prisoners, and many other projects with no resemblance to the comparatively polite world of integrated education. The most skilled trust officials have deep and flexible contacts across the political and social range, often reaching into places and groups that frighten off the more conventional.

Anthony Tomei of the Nuffield Foundation says, 'My admiration for the parents, and indeed the teachers in those early stages, is just unbounded. Amazing. One of the things that inspired trustees here was the thought that here were these groups of parents and teachers who were willing to take these terrific risks, in the face of all the difficulties of the time. That in itself made them think it was worth doing.' Stephen Pittam's philosophical reflection on the bitter arguments that began in the very earliest days about the possibilities of establishing the first school, Lagan, then continued about pushing on to start more schools within a few years, was 'like all good peace movements, there was a split'. When what Pittam describes as the inevitable split happened, and for some considerable time thereafter, Tomei found himself mediating.

Lagan was no sooner recognised by DENI as viable and given financial support, or so it seemed to some of the founders, than three new schools opened on the same day. There followed a further batch of schools, a development that left relationships between many pioneers in tatters. The root of the trouble was simple enough. ACT was a small group whose membership stayed more or less unchanged throughout its history, devout Christians in the main, socially conservative and increasingly outpaced by events. When Tony Spencer's vision of a strategy for integrated education left ACT gasping, the Belfast Charitable Trust for Integrated Education (BELTIE) was formed in October 1984, supported by a number of parents determined to launch the two Hazelwood schools, a pimary and a secondary, in autumn 1985 in north Belfast. At the same time, another group of parents launched a second primary in south Belfast.

In Spencer, the new movement had someone widely recognised as 'a visionary', as one outsider recognised at the time. 'But visionaries are by their nature uncomfortable for others.' The fundamental differences were about the pace of development, scale of ambitions for a new sector, and, to some extent, disagreement about the centrality of commitment to a Christian ethos for the schools, though Spencer shared a deep religious commitment with the rest of the original ACT.

ACT by and large had been nervous about establishing Lagan, then became intent on consolidating it. Members were wary of alienating government support or needlessly, as they saw it, antagonising the other sectors at a time when schools, largely controlled, were being closed because of falling rolls. Some saw another element in the group's caution. 'They were worried about the big voluntary grammars who had Catholic pupils. They thought those would become integrated given time, and they were very keen not to offend them by saying, We have to have proper integrated schools, you're not that,' says one former supporter. 'Places like Methody, Sullivan, Belfast Royal Academy, the Rainey in Magherafelt. Campbell, even. Those were their sort of schools, big names, old money. It was class, really, but they probably didn't recognise that.'

The BELTIE inclination by comparison was to expand, make demands and push government into supporting new schools, in the belief that the desire of parents for integrated education must be met. 'Spencer and company were expansionists,' says an observer who was more sympathetic to the newer group as activists but aware of 'a certain amount of messiness'.

Bystanding in different capacities was difficult while tensions flared, and those obliged to be in the centre beside the disputants felt the strain most. The Nuffield and Rowntree trusts' initial involvement, plus that of other smaller trusts who funded aspects of development, coincided with the most turbulent period of the story. 'All the schools were acting independently,' Anthony Tomei recalls, 'underpinned by rivalries and animosities: it was the most difficult thing to deal with. Much more difficult than DENI, much more difficult than the particular problems of individual schools. Here were two groups of people, with all these qualities I've talked about, dedication and all of that, but who simply didn't talk to each other. I found myself acting as a kind of go-between, sitting down at a meeting with All Children Together, and saying my friends at BELTIE say this, and they'd say "Do they? That's outrageous." Or "We didn't know that." Or vice versa.' Another trust official years later recalled trying to use a gentle version of carrot-and-stick, offering to increase grants if there was collaboration on a new primary school. 'The outcome was that two schools were established, both got their grants, but there was little by way of collaboration!'

As further groups of parents emerged, intent on forming more schools, the tangle became ever more complicated. There were stormy meetings, hurt feelings, and anger that can still be all too easily rekindled by an incautious or ill-judged reference to decisions taken then. For relatively uninvolved but sympathetic witnesses, there was one consolation: none of the argument had to do with religious or political difference. One witness remembers an encounter at the time with a writer eager for details of the latest angry exchange because he had roughed out a play about a group setting up an integrated school. 'And of course the minute they fall out they split down the middle, orange and green,' he said gleefully. He was plainly disappointed, though not discouraged in his project, to learn that no such splits occurred.

Nuffield, being by far the largest benefactor, was able to broker the establishment of a 'treasurers' group' for all the groups setting up schools. A central figure was the academic Alan Smith, one of the founders of the Mill Strand Primary School in Portrush, County Antrim, widely credited with having the skills and the ability to take a more detached view which produced a way out of disagreement and drift. The treasurers' group eventually produced the current coordinating and funding groups: NICIE, and the funding mechanism, IEF.

'Some of the trusts were taking stock of their role,' says one official. 'Where was this leading? For how long might the demands remain? Was it healthy that Great Britain-based trusts had such an influence over the future of integrated education?' The Nuffield and Rowntree trusts, against their own practice and history, endowed the IEF in 1992 to kick it off as Belfast-based, to make it possible to attract further funding from Europe, and so that it might fund the development of schools from within Northern Ireland. The decision came after considerable thought and prolonged discussion.

For one alarmed well-wisher at the time, 'it was the trusts, and in particular Anthony Tomei, that kept the show on the road'. The professionalism of outsiders, with enough of a stake in the project to be universally recognised as impartial and well-meaning, was a relief to many involved, either worn by increasingly personal recriminations or shocked witnesses to an apparently insoluble running quarrel. Government reactions were typically slow-footed. There were months, even years according to some involved, when DENI officials still behaved as though ACT was the moving force in an integrated education movement it had long since left to the newer BELTIE and others who were setting up new schools.

As far as those at the Northern Ireland end are concerned, the story of trust involvement in integrated education has no downside whatsoever. Nor has any local voice been raised against them, a remarkable fact in a place where outside elements routinely have their bona fides disparaged. Charitable trusts have given to so many in Northern Ireland, across such a range of polictical opinion, that bad-mouthers are hard to find. Even some who would blithely offer criticism out of habit are constrained by the knowledge that if not they themselves, then some group close to them will have benefited from the generosity of a trust or trusts.

GOVERNMENT

The NIO tone about integrated education was always predominantly supportive while expressing careful respect for the existing sectors. Turning verbal support into hard cash required some fancy footwork and government willingness to be seen as open supporters. The first minister in Stormont to show some interest was the Tory Nicholas Scott, but the most dynamic assistance came from a much more abrasive man. Suddenly integrated education activists were knocking on an open door: inside was Brian Mawhinney, an evangelical Protestant from Northern Ireland, the first local man sent back by a Tory adminstration to be a direct rule minister.

'It didn't do much for integrated schools in the other sectors that they were Mawhinney's babies,' one expert onlooker remarks, adding with a sigh, 'though they weren't liked anyhow, and they're not liked now.' Mawhinney may have been the most disliked of ministers in the opinion of civil servants, those in the education world who had to deal with him, and the media who found themselves buttonholed by a politician convinced his star was on a sharp upward trajectory from this minor Belfast posting. 'Doesn't matter, he was the key person,' says one insider. 'It goes back to the officials,' says a witness. 'He just basically trod all over them. Said don't give me that, I want this done.'

In contrast to the positive local image of the role of the trusts, government intervention or lack of intervention has attracted criticism on many occasions. The original appeal of the idea of integrated schooling drew on the sense that these were parents 'doing it for themselves', painting walls, turning disused buildings into schools. Nowadays, however, there is some resistance in the public mind to promoters of the section, which may come in part from the widespread awareness that government supports integrated education, and that far from being a humble, modest movement of struggling volunteers, this is a worthy but to many minds essentially marginal cause, with friends who are well-placed and influential.

Among veteran enthusiasts, attitudes are mixed, even confused, about the latest stage of development and the degree to which integrated schools have become the darlings of big-name supporters. Some are extremely proud to have admirers who are famous, wealthy and powerful. Others would still prefer to see themselves as more outside the tent than in, and are critical that the authorities do not deliver more.

One considered verdict from an academic expert more well-disposed to the sector than not is that official support has been patchy and contradictory: government practice has been 'well-intentioned but reactive, lurching from one thing to the next without knowing what they were really getting themselves into, especially financially'. Even in the minds of a number among those most closely involved, the jury is out on whether the nature of official assistance has done the cause more harm than good. This is friendship, a number would judge, much sought after and, in some quarters, much prized, but which may have been damaging overall.

An MA thesis in January 2001 by Ray Mullan, now NICIE's chairman, found that government had been 'slow to concede the rights of those who wanted to choose integrated schools'. It is an opinion supported by several in integrated schools, who think that support has been inadequate, far from 'proactive' as they insist it should be. Others recall that various ministers have offered support at crucial moments and that their help should be recognised: the Tory minister Brian Mawhinney and Sinn Féin's Martin McGuinness are singled out for praise. 'Governments haven't done that much, they've run away from vested interests,' says a principal in one breath, while in the next comes the comment, 'Mind you, Mawhinney did something major.'

Integrated education campaigners have the necessary single-mindedness, born of true single-issue interest, to focus on the usefulness of supporters rather than their flaws. Other observers are less disposed to accept, for example, that Mawhinney's support for integrated education came from a deep-seated and personal commitment to an ideal, rather than from a fairly mainstream and traditional unionist dislike of the Catholic sector. Several veteran reporters remember Mawhinney convening a lunch to broach setting up a Stormont lobby system. Nothing more was heard of the lobby, but from a discussion of the Catholic hierarchy's successful opposition to shared teacher-training, some of the audience vividly recall the minister's boast that the bishops had met their match in him.

Devolution of some power to Stormont initially put the question of integrated schools into the hands of Sinn Féin, political wing of the IRA. A seasoned campaigner and governor of several integrated schools saw Martin McGuinness, appointed Sinn Féin minister for education in 1999, as the new white hope, a pivotal figure in the evolution of political republicanism intent on making a success of the party's controversial choice of the education ministry. Many are nervous that support from McGuinness might cost them sympathy for integrated education, though some remain impressed, like the busy governor who believes that the Sinn Féin minister has a real interest in integration. A number admit that his chief attraction is the possibility that like Mawhinney he might override official caution, and reorder priorities to help the sector expand.

When he lowered viability criteria for groups wanting to start two types of school, Irish-language medium and integrated, McGuinness certainly showed warmth to both. In early 2002, he talked approvingly of integration, admitting easily that the community he came from had once seen it 'like the Alliance Party, as Northern Ireland Office inventions – and maybe there was a degree of truth in that, in the support for it at any rate'. But his perceptions had changed; he said the Good Friday Agreement made it a duty to encourage and facilitate integration, and that 'the track record of integrated schools is very very good, very robust – anyway, I like that form of education'. These were reasons enough for lowering the criteria: 'The question is, do you think it can make a worthwhile contribution to our society, where there has been a bitter conflict? Parents at the forefront of the movement, some believe it can make a very powerful contribution to the resolution of sectarian attitudes and old enmities. And from what I have seen, their motivation is nothing but good. I'm very impressed.'

Those bedazzled by the madeover republican are equally nervous at the prospect of an unsympathetic future home-grown minister. McGuinness expressed a wish to stay in the job beyond the 2003 election, though it was clear that if the DUP emerged as the largest party they would have first choice of departments. Like Ulster Unionists, only much more vociferously, the Reverend Ian Paisley's party expressed constant shock and opposition to

McGuinness the former IRA leader as minister for schools. Some thought this would oblige the DUP to make education their first choice. For the integrated education lobby, the nightmare would be the DUP's Sammy Wilson, as Wilson himself was well aware. In an interview for this book, he chuckled at the description without further comment.

Several insiders record that civil servants in various departments have been remarkably imaginative, even creative, in the ways they have found to help integrated schools. One secured major support for the IEF from the European Union: 'I don't know how he did it,' says an appreciative onlooker. Another civil servant, much earlier, suggested that schools pay rent for premises, which they could be helped with by government, rather than pay interest on bank or trust loans for which no official help would be available. 'Now that was creative thinking,' a witness comments.

Some list interventions, help and advice from officialdom dating all the way back to the earliest days and going right to the top. Cecil Linehan of ACT describes the late John Benn, at one point the most senior official in DENI, encouraging her to apply for funding for Lagan, but admitting that the application process had not yet been drafted. 'He said, "What are you waiting for" – the numbers had gone up from 28 to 56 to I think it was about 121. And I said, "How do you mean what are we waiting for?" He said, "Why don't you apply for funding?" And I said, "How do you do it?" He said, "I don't know, it hasn't happened in my time." I thought they had a form that you would fill in and there wasn't. So this letter went in and we got help with drafting and we pinned to the back of it every single primary school that the kids were coming from.' Benn's personal sympathy was very clear to her. Another recalls dealing with officials and coming away thinking 'there's not much natural sympathy for us there'.

But on reflection, a number of those who now deal with officials on behalf of integrated schools admit that ministerial direction in coming years is likely to be coloured less by personal sympathy or distaste than by a general assessment of educational needs and realities, including falling school rolls and the pressing question of how to rationalise superfluous pupil places. Several of those most involved in fundraising and lobbying for integrated schools are still confident that very senior officials are personally supportive, and convinced that this support can and will shape policy. Occasional gaps do open up, however, between supposed support and the realpolitik of the civil service.

When officials asked in 2002 what activists saw as their final goal and what percentage of schools they hoped would be integrated eventually, 'they were aghast to be told that the dream was for a single entirely integrated system', one activist reports. Officials, however friendly, can only help so far, the most realistic of campaigners admit. If parents are to have the choice of integration, education authorities must take a more strategic approach, Ray Mullan's 2001 paper declares. The overall effect of government policy, he finds, has been 'to obstruct the demand for new schools, while providing a vehicle which has delivered little progress in the transformation option'. Raising a subject many integration supporters have begun to find seriously worrying, he calls for an effective strategy to help existing controlled schools which opt through transformation to change their status and which seek recognition as integrated. It may mean, he says, 'establishing clear support structures to ensure the quality of transformation, including the complex cultural change within a school from single to shared identity status'.

TRANSFORMATIONS

The formal language of Mullan's paper masks a pressing concern. His is a cautious and considered version of a fear much voiced among teachers and supporters of various kinds, throughout most of the older integrated schools and from one end of the support organisations to the other. 'It's a totally political thing,' says a founder governor of an integrated school in County Fermanagh, echoing integrated teachers and governors across Northern Ireland. 'It's bad for us, it's bad for the credibility of integrated education. It's going to be a big big problem in coming years.' Many believe that government intervention in the development of integrated education, in the shape of providing for the transformation of existing controlled schools, may have done serious and irreparable damage.

The government move was justified as a way of swiftly and surely providing more places in integrated education, and more opportunity for parents to choose integrated schools – but mainly the case was that it made economic and managerial sense. There are those in the integrated world who concede that from time to time their project has been flavour of the month in government, but who also recognise the vagaries of official interest. 'I remember,' says one weary campaigner, 'how Michael Ancram [Conservative minister in the NIO under Sir Patrick Mayhew in the mid-1990s] put a moratorium on capital spend – in response, he said, to increased violence when the IRA ceasefire broke down. Hence the raising of criteria for greenfield schools in 1996, and the accent on transformation.' The integrated sector's coffers were steadily drained as a result, trying to keep afloat three new schools launched when government policy was more friendly: the secondaries Ulidia (Carrickfergus, County Antrim) and Strangford (Carrowdore, County Down), and the primary Oakwood (Derriaghy, just south of Belfast).

In 2002, the breakdown revealed that thirteen of forty-seven integrated schools were 'controlled integrated' (see Appendix 2). In other words, they began life as controlled schools, mainly Protestant in enrolment, staffing and management, and won their 'integrated' tag when their parent bodies voted to opt for transformation. No maintained/Catholic school has as yet sought transformation, nor does that seem likely in the foreseeable future. In the meantime, official encouragement has created a whole new sub-division of integration from formerly mainly Protestant schools. The development has meant swift growth in the total of schools deemed integrated, and might well be the main direction of integration in the future. The outlook may change if recent remarks by Martin McGuinness (see Chapter 6), suggesting he is looking afresh at the transformation route, indicate real commitment to a different tack. Few can feel confident of that, however. The course of Northern Ireland's still new power-sharing arrangement has been erratic and Mr McGuinness's tenure of education a matter of recurrent resentment among unionists: whatever his intentions, he may find himself unable to carry them out or may even lose the post after the next election.

It is hard to escape the conclusion that until Mr McGuinness's arrival, official policy was determined not to discover failure and that monitoring was postponed repeatedly to give transforming schools the maximum time for progress. Perhaps no more than was proper, Mr McGuinness diplomatically suggests. There is no official provision for removing transformed status, however. Some try to put on a brave face, but worries outweigh optimism.

One bruised supporter, keen to see the sector expand but un-nerved by the slowness with which largely Protestant school enrolments, staffs and ethos have changed in several schools, concludes, 'It takes a long time to get it through the system. If you start off with your first intake after transformation being only 10 per cent Catholic in your first year, it's going to take at least seven years to get that through the school. You're going to say to people there is integrated education in this area but you've got to change the habits of a lifetime, gradually change governors, teachers, pupils. It probably is damaging, if nothing apparently has changed.'

A resolutely positive veteran insists, 'This is a transitional stage. These schools are in a process now, they're at the beginning of it. They're changing and they'll change more. We have to not be pious about this.' Another longtime supporter comments, 'It might not turn out the way we'd like it to. But won't these still be children and teachers whose experience is very different to that of an ordin-ary controlled school?'

Discussion in the wider integrated world about transforming schools tends to snag on several awkward points, the most enduring being that there is what many judge to be inadequate contact between the different types of school. 'Only one transforming principal ever comes to our meetings,' says one after another principal of 'greenfield site schools', now the favoured term for those integrated schools started by parents. Meetings of the Association of Principal Teachers of Integrated Schools (APTIS) are a popular safety valve for many, a protected environment in which they can discuss the problems they have with boards of governors and perhaps with staff and parents. Invitations sent to transforming heads are apparently not taken up. The conclusion that the newer form of school wants to keep a distance is fed when the bulk of transforming teachers fail to turn up at training days run for the integrated sector by NICIE, or for the Teachers' Committee meetings that others find a useful bonding mechanism.

'Transformation – An Information Pack for Schools' is a beautifully written document, which contains an impeccable list of 'key areas' which 'might require detailed attention' in schools' plans: management, to include reconstitution of boards of governors; organisation, meaning such issues as school name, uniform, badge, and policy on flags and emblems; curriculum review of areas such as 'religious education, sport, music and cultural awareness'; awareness-raising for governors and parents, and pastoral care for pupils; and in-service training for staff. The trouble is that there is no clear timetable for invigilation of movement on all or any of the above.

'Schools must demonstrate the ability to achieve a minimum of 10% of their 1st year intake drawn from the minority tradition (Protestant or Roman Catholic) within the school's enrolment and the potential to achieve a minimum of 30% in the longer term.' So say the DENI criteria for assessing development proposals, which DENI must be given and must approve before the balloting of parents begins. The sceptical wonder how such ability and potential can be demonstrated. 'The Department will initiate a progress review after no more than 5 years to assess progress towards an acceptable religious balance (i.e. reasonable numbers of Catholic and Protestant pupils) in enrolments, intake, staff and Governors, changes in the curriculum and the development of the transformation process in the school as a whole.' The word 'initiate' allows considerable leeway.

Informal contacts that assess staff motivation seem to satisfy the criteria: phone calls and meetings between NICIE and IEF personnel and civil servants in DENI, often at senior level, sometimes informal and in the margin of other meetings. There are concerns and doubts which are widespread; specific transformed schools are widely regarded in their localities as not having changed in ethos, staffing or substantially in enrolment. But the prevailing official will is to tolerate, perhaps even to turn a blind eye for a generous period. The dominant view in integrated education's support groups may be that transformation for many is bogus, but they have held back from saying so in public. In particular, though off the record many scoff, they have not demanded that government police more effectively, or that it should revoke recognition.

It is perhaps the central weakness in the official approach, that integration in ethos and curriculum is described as achievable only through a gradual process, but that integrated status is 'granted' as soon as the transforming school successfully ballots parents and has a development proposal officially approved. Bureaucracies every-where are slow to revoke their own acclamation.

Even those involved in integrated education who are most scep-tical recognise that the motivations of transforming schools differ, though they share the public belief that the most common motiva-tion is to improve enrolment or stave off closure. Running through the list, the well-informed tick off other, sometimes overlapping, reasons in specific cases: desire to improve the school's image covers several, as does adjustment to demographic change, that is, a steady fall in local Protestant numbers. Integrated status has come to mean social elevation to many, as a change to co-education does for secondary schools that were previously boys-only, or so school managements think.

The original concern in the wider integration movement was with the method by which schools transform, and the passions which that often reveals. 'The vote alone,' says the doggedly opti-mistic longtime supporter, 'the fact that so many parents and governors support the idea – that has to mean something, doesn't it?' The more pessimistic, or more clear-sighted, view is that several schools have transformed against considerable internal opposition, among parents, staff and governors. A number of supporters and teachers in greenfield schools draw the same conclusion: that schools now designated as integrated contain people opposed to that concept – parents and, perhaps more damagingly because a more permanent element, teachers. Potential friends in time, or foes inside the camp?

A supporter of integrated education, a parent and governor in the past, looks unhappily at the former controlled secondary school near her home, which seems entirely unconvincing to her as an integrated school. 'Only did it because they had a bad reputation for sectarianism and loyalist vandalism, but I can't see how with this image they'll get many more Catholics.' Her claim was that a predominantly Protestant staff still had strikingly few Catholics. Yet other veterans were enormously impressed by what they knew of the school, and in particular the principal. 'Took on the UDA,' said one, referring to the biggest of the loyalist paramilitary groups, the Ulster Defence Association. 'Has a much wider perspective than usual here on the whole question of minorities,' said another. 'Very convincing on the pointlessness of teaching Irish, for example.' A more sceptical listener thought by contrast that in a solidly Protestant, strongly loyalist area where offering Irish would be instantly controversial and unpopular, this seemed less likely to be evidence of radical thinking than a convenient rationalisation.

This was a sizeable school, however, where the decision to go for transformation might have been influenced by a desire to improve the image, but could not have been attributed to fear that it would otherwise close. Several tiny schools by contrast feed scepticism, though the optimists still cling to the belief that by declaring for formal integration they show a genuine wish to reflect the two main traditions equally, whatever the breakdown of their enrolment. The numbers and the balance invite pessimism from some, even though such schools may build on a long-standing history.

Carnlough, the tiny County Antrim primary with four or five Catholics out of thirty, has a good relationship with the nearby much larger Catholic primary. This is partly to the credit, of course, of both principals but also draws on local folk memory. Ian McKay, employed by NICIE as an outreach worker with several transforming schools, relays with affection the story that Carnlough was originally a deliberately interdenominational quarry school, set up by the quarry-owners: 'The tale is that a Catholic, it might have been a priest, had been taking a hedge school a few miles out of the village and when the school for the workers started, they asked him to come down and teach in it and save himself and his pupils getting wet. So it started out integrated if you like, then it was a state school, and now it's reverted.'

The schools which most convince insiders that they are taking transformation seriously and making headway against considerable local odds are Brownlow (see Chapter 6) and Bangor Central Primary. Bangor Central, enrolment almost five hundred, is a size-able primary in the County Down town that to many in Northern Ireland is a striking example of detachment, a Protestant and unionist place determined to ignore the messiness of nearby Belfast and, as far as possible, the upheaval of post-Agreement politics. In this light, by attempting the transformation process the town's long-established controlled primary has made the most consistent effort of any traditional institution to widen horizons. What is even more remarkable, is that it is not an isolated phenomenon. As ripples spread from the general demographic shifts, and the town's predominantly middle-class make-up continues to diminish with the growth of sprawling down-market estates, other local schools are also changing.

Bangor Central's decision to transform was a recognition of the fact that the town's Catholic population is growing. Some onlookers think there may also have been a judgement that the incomers, having chosen to live in a mixed area, will increasingly look for an integrated school. The enrolment still contains comparatively few Catholics. In the intake for the school year 2002–2003, however, the school was pleased to have twelve Catholic new pupils in a total of seventy-two, a considerably higher proportion than the 10 per cent annual minimum share of intake recommended to produce the ultimate ideal balance. On the outskirts of the town, two

Catholic schools have considerably higher proportions again of Protestant pupils.

A well-run primary draws children against the odds from a neighbouring hardline loyalist estate, because parents prefer it to the estate's controlled primary. The Catholic secondary, St Columbanus' College, is even more popular with Protestant parents because by common local consent it far outshines Bangor's controlled secondary options. It now has an enrolment said to be almost 60/40 Catholic/Protestant, a balance unmatched by any of the schools that have opted to transform. Like other Catholic schools which have also begun to attract Protestant pupils, though in much smaller numbers, there is no suggestion that St Columbanus' College will wish to realign to the integrated sector. The pattern of recent educational choice in Bangor can only be described as surprising, and above all fluid. No sector can be certain of the outcome.

Against this background, Bangor Central's efforts to transform might look less striking. But according to advisers in the sector, despite its still predominantly Protestant parent body the school has steadily expanded its horizons, with teachers working on an inter-schools religious education syllabus project, 'New Sacraments', and the school hosting a conference led by a Catholic nun. Small beer in other parts of the world, perhaps, but a major advance in what has always been one of the most self-satisfied and conservative corners of Northern Ireland.

Other would-be transformers inspire less cheer. One primary looks set to close in the next year or so, having failed, once declaredly integrated, to attract Protestant children back to an estate once largely Protestant but now all but completely Catholic. Another nearby may go for transformation in the same timescale. Both are reacting to considerable local demographic change, where housing estates once predominantly Catholic or Protestant and also plagued by social and paramilitary problems have changed their sectarian complexion, and to some extent also improved as places to live. In both cases, the shift left two controlled schools facing falling rolls and the need to reinvent themselves. It remains to be seen if the second effort fares better than the first.

No structure exists to monitor the 'complex cultural change' Ray Mullan describes as essential if controlled schools are to become truly integrated. Some sincere and knowledgeable supporters of integration look at transformation to date, and come close to despair. 'It's like trying to graft on to integrated education a foreign body,' says a serious-minded teacher who has spent most of the past twenty years in the integrated sector. 'I don't know how that's being dealt with at the minute, but I can see glaring problems.'

A principal teacher in one of the earliest integrated schools refused to discuss transformation, beyond a swift dismissal: 'It doesn't mean anything at all – it's only a matter of numbers, a totally shameless business. Most of them keep the rest of us at arm's length once they've got their new status.' The suggestion was that a serious discussion was only possible if it stayed away from the subject of transformation. Another senior teacher said, before changing the subject with finality, 'If transformation was meant to be a friendly measure on the part of government, perhaps outright hostility would be preferable.'

PARTY FRIENDS

Passions are less strong on the subject of party political friendship for integration, in part because the idea is cloudy for many. A section of supporters is very political indeed, and very aware of the political issues involved. The bulk in their own minds might well be apolitical. There are inside Northern Ireland those who feel they have no way of making a political difference, who badly want to cut across or circumvent in some way the existing balance of power. Starting an integrated school, or sending your child to one, is a way 'not to feel disenfranchised', as several of those most active as parents, governors and fundraisers say.

For some of the least politically involved as well as for some of the most active, signing their children up for integrated schools can be a way of making a personal statement, and some are encouraged by support at home and from abroad to believe that this might be effective politically. In March 2002 an 'Integrated Education Week' was held, though schools varied considerably in the degree to which they marked or contributed to it. Michael Wardlow, chief executive of NICIE, made a deliberately declaratory statement:

> If we are to create a society that is truly integrated, we owe it to our children to dispel the myth about the 'other'. The thousands of parents who have chosen integrated schools have openly declared themselves to be unwilling to simply continue to be a part of history, but to be history makers. Integrated Education Week is a celebration of their achievement as well as an advertisement for what is yet to be delivered.

The structure of the integrated education world is such that Wardlow's lofty declaration was unlikely to have been cleared with anyone. As most who are involved know, there is no organic integrated education 'sector' with tightly defined lines of communication. Some are content, even delighted, with cheerleading, the more high-flown the better. Others 'in the sector' find it alienating, even distasteful, while outsiders divide swiftly into those who raise derisive eyebrows but make no comment, those who bristle, and those who think it an inspirational and totally appropriate line to adopt.

The cross-community Alliance Party is the most high-profile of political supporters, and has the most long-lasting overlap with prominent activists in integrated schools and lobbying: perhaps the best-known being ACT founder Cecil Linehan, Alliance founder member Sir Bob Cooper, who has been a Lagan parent and governor and now chairs the IEF, and the present Alliance president Colm Murray-Cavanagh, who is also a director in NICIE. In the Alliance literature for the June 2001 general election, integrated education and mixed housing shared top billing as 'the way to build a new shared Northern Ireland'. Among the many statements Alliance has made on the subject, the party has hotly rejected criticism of the sector with the assertion that 'integrated education is one of the best ways of creating mutual understanding in a divided society from an early age'.

In the eyes of many who are either critical of or less than enthusiastic about integrated education, Alliance endorsement is predictable and does the sector no good. These are people who dislike Alliance, a party less admired than might be expected for its resolute antisectarian stance and determination to find a peaceable middle way. Some of these people are committed unionists or nationalists, who find Alliance dislikeably tepid, and more superior about bigger and more effective parties than is seemly in the unsuccessful. Some are pleased to see its vote hover around 7 to 8 per cent, apparently terminally.

Colm Murray-Cavanagh says of Alliance, 'I joined in early 1998 just before the Good Friday Agreement,' he says, 'many years after my involvement had begun with integrated education. I selected Alliance because of its support for actual reconciliation such as in integrated education – and because of the clear need for political muscle to put integrated education firmly on the political agenda.' A considerable number in the integrated education world welcome the party's support, making the unanswerable point that bigger parties have not rushed to embrace them. But it is Alliance support, and the identification some make between Alliance and integrated education, which most exercises opinion outside the movement on its choice of friends. A striking number of people involved in integrated schools, both teachers and parents, raise the question of this public perception with disquiet. They also complain that internal identification of the Alliance brand of politics and integration shows a lack of imagination, perhaps even a contradiction.

'I was thinking about talking to you,' an experienced teacher in an integrated school said, 'and I looked out some papers in advance. One was a 1998 document from NICIE and here's something it said. "In the Forum election of 1996 there were at least 25 different parties/groups standing for election – however, over 80 per cent of the electorate voted for one of the four main unionist or nationalist parties." And I thought, so what? There is nearly a feeling within integrated education that it should be the Alliance party at school. I don't think that's what we should be about at all. It seems to me that's a very damaging impression to be putting out. It should be far more diverse than that.'

A woman whose roots are in rural mid-Ulster, where Alliance has never flourished, confesses with slight embarrassment that she 'almost turned away from the schools because I disliked the Alliancey tone I got from some of their spokesmen and -women. It's the holier than thou bit. In the end I didn't let it get to me, and of course when you get involved you realise there's all kinds among the parents, and teachers too. Which is as it should be. We had an Orangeman in our founding group, and there's at least one strong republican among the parents now, very active and keen too.'

Some were pleased to note that the newer, small political groups that emerged in the post-ceasefire, pre-Good Friday Agreement negotiations included strong supporters for integrated education in the Women's Coalition and the small loyalist paramilitary fringe parties. This was preferable to 'holier-than-thou' Alliance backing, some reckoned, and also better fitted a new mood, perhaps a new wave of parents. 'There's a world of difference between these new muscular nonsectarians,' says one political observer, 'and insipid Alliance types. They used to determinedly find a fence and sit upon it: they believed the numbers of nice people would grow and be the ones to actively push the big sectarian blocs towards agreement, or alternatively they'd act as a catalyst for agreement. But that's not what happened.'

When the Progressive Unionist Party (PUP) spokesman Billy Hutchinson publicly endorsed integrated education, not once but repeatedly, it began to give integrated schools in Belfast a new image in some working-class Protestant eyes. Hutchinson made public the fact that he had sent his son to Hazelwood Integrated College: the school duly built up a Shankill Road following. However, the Progressive Unionists may already have peaked, and their highest total of votes is still below the Alliance party's least successful showing. Their origins as spokesmen for the paramilitary Ulster Volunteer Force were unpromising, and continued paramilitary violence was damaging and ultimately destructive of the fringe parties' attempt to create a constructive image for deprived Protestant districts. Nevertheless, the personal magnetism and political instincts of Hutchinson and his colleague David Ervine convinced many that there was more to loyalist gunmen than mindless thuggery. The hope, almost destroyed by murderous feuding in the last few years between loyalist groups, is that Ervine's and Hutchinson's short-lived provision of a nonsectarian voice for working-class unionism will at some stage be repeated in districts like the Shankill, but this time tied to sound political organisation. A link with integrated education might just be one lifeline for that prospect.

VISITORS

In the meantime, schools like Hazelwood, Malone College on the line where south meets west Belfast, Dungannon's second-level school and several others give the lie to the accusation that integrated education is 'only for the middle class' and is wholly sited in middle-class districts. Like others in the sector, these schools tend to welcome friendship and approval wherever it is offered. Visitors are a major feature in many integrated schools: famous visitors, royal visitors, 'distinguished strangers', and VIPs. From early in its history, Lagan became a staple in the itinerary for visiting academics, journalists in search of a good news story between stints covering paramilitary violence or failed political initiatives, and dignitaries of one kind or another. The last have been arguably the most damaging to general perceptions, though, at least initially, many involved in integrated education welcomed almost any publicity, seeing it as essential support for a risky new venture.

There is certainly a strong disposition abroad to see integrated education as the one reliable bit of good news out of war-torn Northern Ireland, a tale of hands across the peacelines. The world's media have tended to truck around integrated schools almost as relaxation. Since the peace process began, the new routine includes a visit to an integrated school to demonstrate what reconciliation might look like, in time.

The practice undoubtedly feeds already primed resentment among state and Catholic schools. Principals and some education officials complain that when the integrated sector is endlessly depicted as the model of how to overcome Northern Ireland's divisions, the other sectors are effectively portrayed by default as fomentors of sectarianism. 'Why don't they just sketch in the helipad and be done with it?' one controlled school head asked waspishly, as he caught sight of the plans for a new integrated school – years after the school had begun in down at heel mobile classrooms, but way too early in the mind of jealous nearby schools in the older sectors. 'Novelty's the thing,' the peeved head said. 'There isn't a VIP hits town but the Northern Ireland Office has them trekking up to Lagan or dropping into Hazelwood.'

Few deny that, indeed, the civil service and government disposition is to route visiting bigwigs towards the newer kind of school, and the peace process may even have upped the tempo. The draw of the integrated sector is unmatchable in media-pleasing, image-making terms: Catholics and Protestants under the same roof displaying the appeal of togetherness; better yet, young and photogenic Catholics and Protestants in easily organised form, willing and able to perform rites of togetherness and forgiveness.

One of the most media-perfect images, much repeated, worried a few inside integration: the spectacle of small children from an integrated primary school at Stormont waving paper doves outside the talks that produced the Good Friday Agreement, hours before the deal was concluded. 'Who had that bright idea, and did anyone think twice before agreeing to it? Too much like Communist China for me,' said a parent of children at a nearby school, also integrated.

Hazelwood College was the first integrated school to invite a VIP from the Republic, an exception in the traditional stream of British royalty and government figures. The arrival of the then Irish president Mary Robinson in Hazelwood happened to coincide with a major political story in Dublin, the beginning of the collapse of a government – and a flock of journalists arrived in Hazelwood to look for a comment from Mrs Robinson. Principal Noreen Campbell willingly admits that the visit also prompted heated discussion inside the school, like the first visit by the Sinn Féin minister for education, Martin McGuinness.

'That was a useful visit,' she says of the McGuinness event, 'and a useful discussion. We didn't ask for it, the suggestion came from the department and was to mark the launch of a computer system. We had no walk-out, that was important. And although some in the staff weren't all that happy, they said their piece in advance and we talked it through. What chance would there have been of the children discussing it peaceably if we as a staff couldn't?'

But the cheery words whisked over what had been a singularly testing time for the school, when Hazelwood at one point faced an approaching march by loyalist schoolchildren demanding that all Protestants walk out of schools to protest against McGuinness as minister for education.

When British and Irish prime ministers Tony Blair and Bertie Ahern flew in for yet another make-or-break session of talks and wanted an off-duty photo opportunity to boost morale, Hazelwood was chosen to be the setting. Noreen Campbell smiles at the memory and the fleeting possibility that the school would be the backdrop to a breakthrough in the talks. She had no qualms about Hazelwood being used by image-makers, judging the image of the two prime ministers appearing relaxed together and exuding friendship to be perfectly in keeping with the school's picture of itself.

She also argues that visitors, perhaps especially those with big names, are a valuable resource for a still new and developing school in a predominantly difficult, deprived district. 'You can't be po-faced about this. Big names are big names. It's good for the school to be associated with success, good for the children's self-esteem.'

In the words of the academic Tony Gallagher, who has taken part in two studies that examined Hazelwood in a group of 'effective schools in disadvantaged areas', there is educational merit in a practice others might see as showboating. 'The intention is that the pupils become aware that the visits are important not only because the visitor is important, but also because the visited are important.'

In the minds of some involved, being high on the rota for VIP visits may smack of becoming established, even ordinary, but the trade-off is worth it. As in other integrated schools, there is a qualified awareness that the media are on balance much more supportive than not, and that the long struggle to establish a new sort of education still needs all the help it can get.

A certain amount of grittiness sticks to Hazelwood College and the nearby Hazelwood Primary, which is in an even more exposed position, simply because they function in troubled north Belfast. But can a reputation as daring or radical be sustained, some on the inside wonder, if yours are the schools on semipermanent show to royalty, repeatedly trotted out by civil servants for the world's approval? Others counter with the reminder that the older sectors have always happily grabbed whatever public ceremonies or visitors they are offered – at least where they supposed their boards and parents would accept them. In this regard at least, the resentment of older schools is easily suffered.

3
Enemies

To some minds, the establishment of a power-sharing devolved administration at Stormont, even though it is part of the slow and erratic arrival of peace, might be a mixed blessing for integrated education. Opportunity comes with a prickly and possibly hostile outer wrapping. As normal community relations become more possible, at least in theory, and innocent or naïve parties imagine that integrating school systems might be the place to begin the work of reconciliation, opponents of the idea will presumably become more resolute and less coy. Integrated education has many friends but also many enemies, not all of them open and declared. Attacking the aim of educating children together has become increasingly difficult if not impossible in mainstream religion and politics. Other routes of criticism are easier, and much travelled. As one lifelong supporter of integration, delighted at seeing it put into practice, says, 'Critics very often dismiss it as something trivial. But then they usually have an agenda.'

The agendas are many. For such an apparently mild proposition, integrated education arouses considerable emotion, all the more striking in many cases because it is concealed, disavowed, or presented as no more than rational, utilitarian argument. Sometimes underlying distaste only becomes apparent when the proponent of integration argues the case, or perhaps even dares to speculate that the opponent is more engaged than rational.

The most upfront enemies have always been religious, a truth that surprises no one close to the education world but is perhaps a shock to gentle souls with the illusion that professing religion should make a person at the least more idealistic, if not inclined to good works. The next layer down, veiled slightly with politeness and a reluctance to be too specific, is made up of people, usually Catholic, who see integrated education primarily as a challenge to the clarity and distinctiveness of political identity. Then there are the even more polite but even less honest opponents who pose as supporters. These people write letters to newspapers or telephone radio programmes to make statements like: 'I support integrated education: I went to an integrated school as do my children. We have fine integrated schools and always have had, provided by the state. If the Catholic Church didn't insist on their own separate schools all would be well, because then Catholic children would come to state schools. Which would then be integrated in fact, as well as legally.'

It is probably simplest to deal with this argument first. It is a frequent argument made by Protestants against a separate integrated sector, that state schools are open to all, and are therefore technically or potentially integrated, though unfortunately they are largely Protestant in enrolment. The absurdity never seems to strike those who so argue, and often leaves listeners silenced by mirth, or by shock at the brazenness of the claim. Highly educated head teachers have been known to claim the tag 'integrated' for schools that have at best a minority of Catholic pupils, rarely if ever acknowledged as such, in fact often required for their own comfort and that of the school to be indistinguishable from the Protestant majority. Schools are sometimes vaunted as integrated that have few if any Catholic teachers and few if any Catholic members of the board of governors.

Tony Spencer, the launching spirit of Lagan College whose four older children attended largely Protestant schools after Catholic primary education, has a fund of memories – the most striking being his son's pretence in school that he was Protestant – which convinced him that 'mixing' fell well short of respectful 'integration'. From the children's Catholic primary school came comments on their 'English accents': remarks about their different pronunciation of the word 'courtesy', he recalled, as precise a definition of discourtesy as could be imagined. In later years, several came home from secondary school with tales of anti-Catholic remarks made by teachers either careless of the feelings of their few Catholic pupils, or unaware of Catholics in their classes. 'You sound like some old choir up the Falls Road,' a music teacher had scolded. '*Je suis Protestant, nous sommes Protestants*', went the blithe conjugation in a genteel girls' grammar school. The Spencer children's experiences, which he credits with helping him to draft a model integrated school, date from the 1970s and 1980s. Few suggest that much has changed since then. From inside and outside the integrated sector alike, many accounts emphasise that even though Catholics are now much more numerous in mainly Protestant schools, silence and cunning are still the watchwords on the touchy questions of religion and political identity.

The incidents that make the news are remarkable only because they become known. In April 1980, the headmaster of the state secondary school in Banbridge, County Down, held a meeting with senior pupils to try to ward off a walk-out in protest against the presence of Catholic pupils. Local tensions were high: a considerable number of police families live in and around strongly Protestant Banbridge, and a few weeks earlier an IRA mortar bomb attack had killed nine officers not far away in Newry police station. One report suggested the unrest had begun over the single Catholic teacher on the staff, but there were also complaints about the number of Catholic pupils. The headmaster would make no comment to the press but told the pupils, it was reported, that people of all religions were entitled to attend the school. The Banbridge incident met with silence, then and since, from the proponents of the argument that the state sector is open to all, therefore integrated, thus there can be no reasonable need for a new sector.

Most Protestant schools absorb their Catholics without the slightest sign that they are there. 'I remember the single Catholic girl in our sixth form,' says a male contemporary, 'because she did so well. She arrived in the middle of the year, which was hard, but she made friends with the right people. The girls were all popular, and because they were her friends a bunch of the rugby boys decided to see that she was all right. She probably had a great time.' But he had no idea how she felt when angry parents removed children from the school choir and turned up to protest at an arrangement made to sing carols with a neighbouring Catholic school in the nearby Catholic church.

Scenes of picketing and dispute are no longer cost-free, even for the hardline. With the IRA's political front in politics and often professing sweet reason, unionist politicians have begun to try and find other ways to make their own least reasonable and most nakedly sectarian cases. Education is comparatively easy to negotiate: they never admitted in the first place that they would prefer separation to stay just as it is. Instead, the fiction has survived that opposition to integration has always come wholly from the Catholic Church, while unionists in general have been stalwart upholders of complete integration, very much regretting the separation of children. A number of unionist politicians maintain the façade of support for integration, usually in defence of arguments against new planned integrated schools, or against the proposed transformation of a state school. In the minds of those who have experienced the 'integration' of Catholic-free schools, the pretence is easily disposed of.

'They want Catholics to come to their schools but to leave their Catholicism and Irishness at the door,' said one Protestant sharply. 'I'd like to hear them say that of course they welcome the arrival of priests to alternate prayers at assembly with the ministers the school already uses, and naturally the school will now mark some Catholic holy days. Plus they'll be off to the Catholic church for one carol concert in three or four, and they'll be inviting prominent nationalists to come and speak on alternate prize days in among all the usual unionist figures, without expecting them to stand for the Queen.' It was clear she did not expect her prescription to be followed, and not only because many teachers would oppose such changes. 'I know that if a Catholic priest stood up in our school hall at assembly, the next morning we wouldn't have a school hall.' The preference of many Protestants for integrated schools is recorded and accepted at face value by polls, but is nowhere widely evident on the ground.

The emergence of an integrated sector stirred up considerable unease, especially in the early 1980s when falling rolls closed a number of Protestant schools and threatened several that were Catholic. The principals of two schools in Portrush wrote to the local education and library board to voice concern about the plan to open an integrated school. The board's education committee voted nine to one to support the principals. There were sufficient schools in the area already and 'several members made the point that controlled schools are in effect integrated schools'.

The deputy Democratic Unionist leader, Peter Robinson, said in May 1985, as speculation began about siting the proposed new Lagan College on his side of Belfast, that he 'was in favour of integrated education', but that the Lagan College experiment would damage the prospect of full integration becoming available through the state. It was the old unionist argument again, that Catholics should be encouraged to abandon their separate schools for state schools. Even the DUP can say, when it chooses, that it is in favour of integration.

In 1994 the principal of a controlled primary school in Dromore, County Tyrone, vocally opposed the proposal to open an integrated secondary school in the Dungannon–Moy area at a meeting of the Southern Education and Library Board. A number of local principals, she claimed, had received 'rather abusive' phone calls from integrated supporters: 'They expect you to drop whatever you are doing to attend to their needs.' Integrated schools, she said, amounted to 'middle-class society being given private education at taxpayers' expense. There can be integrated education without this separate sector. I will take a child irrespective of religion.' A Social Democratic and Labour Party (SDLP) councillor on the board agreed that integrated schools were 'a waste of money'. The school opened that September as Integrated College Dungannon, and now has an enrolment of over four hundred.

Much more crudely, unionist councillors complained long and hard over several years at proposals to transform the Brownlow secondary school in Craigavon, County Armagh. It would mean positive discrimination on behalf of Catholic teachers in future staff appointments, they said. It would mean the loss of a school. In other words, Brownlow might try to employ some Catholic teachers to dilute their wholly Protestant staff, now that they had declared their intention to increasingly mix their enrolment. But the councillors also criticised the Catholic Church's opposition to integrated education. The local branch of the Independent Orange Order deplored 'the sacrifice of Craigavon's only state school to integration'. In this they echoed several clumsy Protestant clerics whose reaction to transforming has been to bewail the fact that 'our' schools will no longer be 'ours'. The usual jumping-off point for Protestant arguments against integration is insistence that state schools belong to all and are not controlled by the Protestant churches. The contradiction in then calling them 'ours' never seems to sink in.

Perhaps the most contorted and obscure Protestant reaction to integration was voiced in the late 1980s, when the Church of Ireland Bishop of Clogher and vice chair of his local education board, Brian Hannon, said the idea of integration being a panacea should be kept in perspective. There was, he went on, a danger of classrooms becoming polarised along sectarian lines if children whose parents were in favour of mutual understanding were removed – clearly, he meant, to new integrated schools. A 1999 pamphlet by the hard–hitting Church of Ireland liberal pressure group, Catalyst, on 'Separatist Education' recounted the performance of the CoI's board of education, highlighting 'how the church, in common with the other churches, has used education … to attack and exclude others and to create division'. Author Duncan

Scarlett, a former head teacher in north Belfast, found that board of education statements on 'Transferors' Rights' – referring to the positions reserved for church representatives on state/controlled school management – 'showed little understanding that these had been achieved' by what he described as cynical and at times openly sectarian campaigns in the 1920s, 1930s and 1940s.

> The use of the words 'our' and 'Protestant' to describe state/controlled schools and phrases such as the 'denominational character ... of our schools' reflects at the very least a proprietorial attitude which is statutorily incorrect, as such schools do not belong to the Protestant denominations. The repeated demands for recognition of Transferors' rights in the management of totally new grant-maintained schools seems more about extending denominational influence or control than seeking participation or partnership.

Though unionist opposition to integrated education tends toward the covert and deliberately obscure, some Protestant opposition to any contact between the sectors is verbal and overt. The Democratic Unionist Party leader the Reverend Ian Paisley once condemned an interschool project in County Fermanagh as a 'romanist indoctrination programme': Paisley is not always careful to separate his pronouncements as Moderator of the Free Presbyterian Church from his comments as party leader. The DUP education spokesman in the Stormont Assembly is Sammy Wilson, a former teacher in the overwhelmingly Protestant Grosvenor Grammar School in east Belfast, and a former Methody pupil, who as a veteran Belfast councillor is a master of pugnacious and embittered public comment. There is no doubting Wilson's hostility to the integrated sector, though he has become slightly more suave over the years.

Wilson's objections are first that the parents who want integrated schools are the snobbish middle class, next that they endanger existing schools. Wilson speaks nowadays as if his concern is equally for Catholic as for state schools, a stance that would surprise anyone who has followed his utterances through the years. He also shies away from the once-popular stonewalling gambit that state schools should be the approved route to integration. Pressed to clarify whether he would welcome Catholic children in controlled schools with a programme to recognise and value their religion and culture, Wilson comes up with an alternative it is difficult to imagine his party leader approving: that there should be no religion in the schools he at first describes, punctiliously as the law describes them, as 'open to all'. The people he speaks for would clearly not tolerate the changes these schools would have to undergo if Catholics chose to pour into them. Rather than that, Wilson says, 'I think maybe you'd be better to have no religion taught. Many people would say religion should be out of schools altogether.' He also declares:

I believe the whole integrated education movement was started by middle-class parents who wanted to make sure of a system they could use to keep their children away from the great unwashed, especially at the secondary level. Maybe their youngsters didn't want to go to the local secondary school so they wanted a separate system and they said we'll call it an integrated system. There's no doubt in my mind that it's an attempt by the middle class to keep their youngsters away from children they think undesirable. You would expect the people who say they support integrated education to put down integrated schools as their first choice. In most cases, and certainly in the early days, it was not so. Nowadays a lot of people might put it down as first choice, probably because they compare the shiny new schools in the integrated sector with the tired old schools in the others.

The DUP's education spokesman voices most of his objections as those of 'many in the controlled sector', who feel, he says, 'that integrated schools have an unfair advantage from the government's desire to promote a new sector'. He adds, somewhat grimly, 'It's time to put them under some pressure, either in terms of free transport or the provision of new schools.' He makes the familiar claims that some integrated schools opened where controlled schools were closed, repeating unsubstantiated allegations that some opened with fewer on the rolls than previous schools closed with.

Failing schools are finding it difficult to compete with integrated schools, he says, citing troubled north Belfast as an example and pointing to the newly built Hazelwood Integrated College as unfair competition for local state and Catholic secondaries: entirely because of its 'shiny' new building, he asserts. 'Many people ask, is this a good way of using scarce education resources – adding another sector when we have a declining school population.' Finally comes the argument that there already are schools open to all: 'A controlled school is open to everyone anyway, and many voluntary schools, for example Methody, are in fact mixed. Methody's sixth form, they say, is half and half.'

Sammy Wilson makes it clear that audible and visible Catholicism in controlled schools is not an option, though without ever saying so. Instead, he elaborates on the unsatisfactory nature of the religion currently available, and notes with clear approval the many protests from parents about the unbiblical nature of religion in controlled schools and other aspects of teaching or school management thought to be 'un-Christian', a feature of Northern Ireland experience familiar to many teachers, though rarely publicised.

Schemes to bring schools into closer contact have also been the target of fierce and unremitting attack by a sizeable section of parents and, less openly, staff. There are umbrella terms for what parents do not like, as Wilson attests. 'In many schools parents don't like what is provided in religion anyhow – it's all ecumenical, almost believing in nothing. Many withdraw their children. I think you'd be better to have no religion taught than that. I'm a bit ambivalent about whether religion should be taught in school or at home by the parents.' The Bible reading groups popular in many controlled schools, with both pupils and members of staff meeting in lunch hours and occasionally after school, come in two broad types: fundamentalist/anti-ecumenical and less so, sometimes considerably less so. Few, if any, schools are inclined to chide internal school Bible groups for criticising 'ecumenists', a term widely used as code for willingness to recognise Catholics as fellow Christians.

Given the abusive criticism that 'ecumenical' Protestant teachers of religion have always taken from fundamentalists, the Reverend Ian Paisley foremost among them, the prospect seems vanishingly remote of the controlled school system, with the cooperation and agreement of staff and Protestant parents, ever becoming fully and genuinely integrated. Given the realities of school life in strongly Protestant districts, schools that have opted to become 'transformed' and that are now avowedly 'controlled integrated', have major questions to answer (see Chapter 4).

Yet, in part because Protestants and unionists sometimes confuse 'experts' and outsiders by professing support for integration, it is Catholic opposition that first leaps to mind for many. Here also, spokespeople have become steadily more suave and less aggressive in manner, as the conflict has wound down and comparative peace begins to make moderation sound essential. A growing sense of competition can breed a sneaky kind of hostility. A Catholic teacher in an integrated school west of the Bann laments that the nearest Catholic school refuses to turn out against his new Gaelic football team. The Catholic sports teacher is a fellow player of Gaelic games: the integrated sports teacher is nevertheless convinced he does not want to see the integrated school field a decent team because it would boost the claim that Irish culture is reflected in the school ethos, and make them a more credible rival. Once, Catholic teacher 'guilds' for the especially devout professional launched forthright attacks in their publications on the 'secularists' of integrated education. The outspoken condemnations of the past have largely gone out of fashion, and been replaced by gentle-sounding emphasis on the merits of an education that puts pastoral care and the development of the whole pupil at the centre.

It must be an important consideration for the Church that Catholic parents are no longer meek and biddable in the matter of education as in the lost battle of contraception. There is also the question of sounding intransigent, even bigoted and narrow. Opposing integration is now more often a matter of defending the merits of Catholic education, rather than an open attack on an inferior system. Considerable remnants of the old psychology are still visible, however. 'Really they would like to say that separation is grand, it's just what they want,' says an unsympathetic teacher in the integrated world. 'But they have to come at it from a different angle. Who can praise the separation of children in this day and age?'

In the 1970s, it was still possible. The late Reverend Michael Dallat, then the head of the Catholic teacher training college for men, St Joseph's, later a bishop and then chairman of the Council for Catholic Maintained Schools (CCMS), wrote:

> Far from doing damage, separate schools may be strengthening the fabric of society. The richness, the strength and ultimately the health of any society comes from diversity not from uniformity. Why should separate schools be any more divisive than athletic and sporting organisations and clubs, trade union and professional groupings or indeed political parties ... One of the state's first functions in education is to protect and promote the rights of parents and not to usurp these rights. The obligation of government is to help parents attain for their children the education the parents want, not the education the government wants.

In 2002, the chief executive of CCMS, Donal Flanagan, hits a somewhat different and considerably more diplomatic note, at least initially. 'We try not to make comments on integrated education,' he says. 'We try to make comments instead on what we're about.' Among bishops and priests, the sole remaining flagellator of the unorthodox and undutiful Catholic parents who opt to send their children to other than Catholic schools, remains Monsignor Denis Faul, retired since 1997 from his job as principal of a large boys' secondary school. Monsignor Faul can still be relied on to roast Catholic parents for choosing integration, and to inveigh against governments for supporting the integrated sector – or as he puts it, promoting it – and against the media and others for boosting the schools.

He is an unrepentant controversialist. Much more outspoken than his superiors, for decades he criticised the British army and Royal Ulster Constabulary (RUC) for allegedly maltreating hundreds of republican suspects in custody or interrogation, criticism which gave him considerable standing in the Catholic community for many years. (Quirky as ever, he has probably forfeited much of what remained of it, having supported the new police service some way in advance of nationalist politicians.) A vintage Faul diatribe in 1989 against integrated education caught the breadth of his grievance, his conviction that the enemies of Catholicism and Irish nationalism are identical and fighting on a broad front.

It was a stance which even then sounded old-fashioned in style, but still had considerable resonance:

> Historically I believe that in Ireland and other colonies freedom was secured by education and not by violence. Contrast the difference between the slaughter of the poor uneducated Irish in 1798 (when the French went home safely and the landlords were spared) with the effectiveness of the struggle in the 20th century when the people had been educated in Catholic schools run by priests, nuns and brothers. The same pattern is observed in Nigeria, Kenya and India.
>
> Governments including the successive administrations in Northern Ireland realise this, and they underfund Catholic education and oppose it by promoting integrated education ... One hears very little of the Catholic nationalist or Gaelic tradition. The whole emphasis is on looking after the Unionist or Protestant tradition. Catholics are expected in the south to adopt laws enabling divorce and abortion, and in all parts of Ireland the urge of the media is for schools without religion or a religious ethos. (*Irish News*, 2 March 1989)

Catholics who did not send their children to Catholic schools 'inflicted a grievous wound on their children', Faul said, depriving them of 'a uniquely precious gift – an education with a 6,000-year-old perspective on religion ... These parents endanger their faith and they are helping to betray the faith of the coming generations by failing to support Catholic schools now. Who gave them leave to opt out of the Catholic community for selfish or snobbish reasons? Their duty is to support Catholic education and strengthen it for the coming generations.'

Monsignor Faul is a warm and charitable man with a wealth of humour and a winning habit in private of launching into swingeing self-deprecation, hard on the heels of accusations of treachery by the effete and weak-minded. It is his practice to declare that parents who choose other than Catholic schools 'break Canon law', though Canon law is not lightly invoked by others in the upper ranks of the Catholic Church in Northern Ireland. This is a Church that has painfully established rules on pronouncements that will be heard beyond their own congregations, hyperaware of operating in a society with a sizeable, often murderous, anti-Catholic element. One senior cleric wrote to newspapers to explain that 'breaking canon law' did not constitute a sin – the prevalent clerical belief is clearly that this is less than effective as a scarifier, at least in public, and that it holds the Church up to ridicule or opens it up for accusations of heavy-handedness and intolerance.

In the early days of integrated education, parents often described how they were visited at home by parish priests urging them, sometimes angrily, to turn away from their choice of integrated education and enrol their child or children in a Catholic school. It is a less common occurrence now, according to a range of parents in recently opened integrated schools, but it still happens.

A much more common style of reaction than Faul's outspokenness, is the chilly response of the aged Dean Francis McLarnon in Dungannon, County Tyrone, in January 1991, when he declined to attend the opening in the town of the new integrated primary school. Other leaders of local churches turned up. Dean McLarnon, a friend of Father Faul who also taught in Dungannon, confirmed that he had received an invitation but said he 'had no involvement in integrated education'.

When Faul returned to the theme in recent years, he himself noted mischievously to many that he was out of fashion. His bishop bumped into him at a social function shortly afterwards and allegedly rolled his eyes, quipping 'Another fine mess you got us into, Denis.' Faul's is the most extreme opposition, but he only voices in politically incorrect form what many others think, and what the more polished and politic write in circuitous language. Where he strikes a particularly popular chord is in twinning Catholicism and nationality as the schools' joint freight. Many of those who know little detailed history are familiar with the aims of public education in earlier centuries. 'The Irish were to be civilised by learning and the contents of the national curriculum had clear social and political intentions … designed to have a social and transformative purpose,' the conflict specialist Seamus Dunn has written of the 1831 national schools (in *After the Reforms: Education and Policy in Northern Ireland*, 1993).

Integrated schools were seen by many nationalists as part of a deliberate 'splintering' of communal identity, Dunn added. It is a deep and almost instinctive reaction. There are many who have much less warmth for the reinforcement of faith through Catholic schools, than they do for the reinforcement of identity. Every duplicitous unionist statement of support for integration adds to a widely shared Catholic conviction that the sector is at bottom a unionist or British ploy to weaken Irishness, anti-unionist distinctiveness, and the determination of an entire political community.

Tony Spencer argued in the mid-1980s that separate schooling had ill effects in Northern Ireland because it worked against the emergence of a shared identity:

> It did not cause the conflict but it did prevent cultural and structural developments that could be expected over two generations to create a conflict resolution system. It directly reinforces segregation in marriage, in work and in housing, in politics, recreation and the mass media: obstructs the emergence of a shared identity, and directly reinforces cultural misconceptions, stereotypes and prejudice. Indirectly it legitimises social discrimination and structural alienation, and undermines the social foundations of potential conflict resolution systems.

This was a typically robust Spencer interpretation of history and political development, written for an academic audience, but in essence repeated at various points when he was interviewed about integrated schools. Spencer irked many unionist educationalists, notably in confrontations in the Belfast Education and Library Board, but he also undoubtedly restoked suspicion among nationalists about education as a political tactic. His assertion that separate schooling legitimised discrimination and structural alienation led many to dismiss him and the section he spoke for as no more than the latest excuse for the Stormont years. Nationalists tended to miss

Spencer's acute analysis of the degree to which Catholics in mainly Protestant schools were perforce assimilated into monocultural, unionist structures. Spencer in turn arguably underestimated the degree to which nationalists would suspect a system presented as a break with history, a new start for both communities.

'Integrated education was a political gimmick originally by unionists to shift blame to the Catholics,' growls the veteran polemicist and labour historian Andy Boyd, a Protestant married to a Catholic, who sees little improvement in recent political developments and believes sectarianism is ineradicable. 'You have to go back to the sixties and early seventies. A political ploy at the beginning, that's what it was, starting with a unionist deputy lord mayor of Belfast saying that Catholics were responsible for community divisions because they insisted on sending their children to separate schools. Then the Northern Ireland Labour Party MP David Bleakley took it up.'

Boyd remembers being invited to a controlled school in north Belfast, possibly in 1970, by an early cross-community group, PACE (Protestant and Catholic Encounter), to take part in a debate on integrated education. As an organiser at that point of labour colleges, he explained to the meeting that he believed in totally secular education, his programme of religious education ideally to be delivered by a clergyman coming into the school once a year. 'But I said, Look round and you can see why Catholics don't want to send children to state schools. There was a picture of the Queen, and an Ulster flag on the school wall.' He recalled blank looks in return.

'Doesn't matter what they say they want, some parents might not even know that's what the underlying thrust is. It was always an attempt to get rid of the Catholic schools and make the state schools the only system. The purpose is to strengthen unionists. They always saw the Catholic sector as political as well as religious, and so it was of course.'

A leading churchman invited the press in Belfast for a rare informal lunch in the early 1990s, and allowed them a glimpse of Catholic Church gut reaction to integration. On an occasion clearly intended to build some kind of sense of personal connection with the media, he was plainly irked at one point by being pushed to justify his personal chilliness towards overtures from the integrated schools about appointing chaplains and recognising the teaching of fundamentals about the sacraments to young children. The standard practice in the diocese was to leave letters unanswered for months, sometimes years, then to conduct an exceedingly formal and unforthcoming meeting, which usually left the integrated education people more confused than before about what, if anything, they had better do next. 'What is it that they want?' the churchman asked his hushed, attentive audience, though it was not the general impression that he looked forward to being given an answer. 'Some kind of *blend*?' He heaped the word 'blend' with great distaste.

Several of those present had no doubt from the tone used that the churchman meant the most vulgar possible form of mixing, as in mixed marriage, as well as, just possibly rather than, a blend of theological belief. It is one of the least sayable objections to integration, but it lurks beneath the surface of conversation with many less doctrinally opposed than that senior Catholic cleric. The 'numbers question' is likely to become steadily more contentious over the next few years. The mood is of mutual wariness, between a vanishing and demoralised Protestant majority and a Catholic population flexing political muscle: old model gone, replacement not yet crystallised. In this light, the integration of education takes on potential extra significance. It was always the most political of issues, which is why much discussion of integrated schooling has an inbuilt element of aggression and suspicion.

Pressure for a poll on the removal of the border and unification of Ireland may well grow from republicans, increasingly confident that the outcome will point towards a united Ireland in the foreseeable future. Unionists may also call for a poll, doggedly insisting that even should they lose their majority, a sizeable proportion of nationalists/Catholics will still vote to stay in the UK. In this atmosphere, institutions that are seen to reinforce rather than dilute political identity, such as separate schooling, may well become more controversial rather than less.

The underlying political reality is of a buoyant Catholic

population, comparatively relaxed about the present and decidedly relaxed about prospects for the future. It is commonly accepted among Catholics, and among Protestants considering the Catholic experience, that a widely shared communal interest in education has paid off. Catholic perceptions of schooling as the ladder out of disaffection, particularly for the less affluent, and as a ladder into affluence for the middle class, are compared by many analysts with the traditional lack of interest towards education displayed in the Protestant working class. Unionist politicians increasingly demand help for the least successful schools in deprived districts to counter newly discovered loyalist alienation, though they have always opposed assistance sought on the same basis for Catholic schools as unwarranted.

The rise of republican politics, and the comparatively successful transition of the IRA from carrying on a ruthless war to the main-tenance of an imperfect but welcome (and valuable) peace, co-incided with loyalist alienation which became visible chiefly in the chaos and crime of the loyalist paramilitary world, and in unpleas-ant, self-destructive loyalist protests. The struggling loyalist fringe parties were the first to argue effectively that inadequate schools held their districts back, and that republican/Catholic attitudes to education were a major factor in the comparative political success of nationalists in general and republicans in particular. But it was obvious that many republicans had benefited from an altogether different kind of education – in jail. By all accounts little of it was inspired by Catholicism.

The selective system which gave free university education to suc-cessive generations of comparatively poor Catholic children left large numbers in struggling secondary schools in the Falls, Creggan, in Newry and Armagh and rural areas. The most prominent figures in the SDLP, the voice of moderate nationalism for much of the past thirty years, have been grammar and university graduates, many of them teachers. Founding leader John Hume, originally a history teacher, liked to trace the rise of a once unpolitical and depressed political grouping to the arrival of free secondary and university education, and he spoke often of his own beneficial experience of passing the eleven-plus in its first year. For a community accustomed to thinking of itself at that stage as second-rate, Hume saw unanswerable virtue in what he interpreted as educational meritocracy, but his party, often referred to as 'the teachers' party', has also always had an antiselection strand.

Catholic/republican opposition to the selective system is somewhat muted by a communal awareness that Hume's leadership came from a class still largely connected to the class it developed from. There is more social cohesion among Catholics than Protestants, some of it attributable to Catholic Church teaching, even more to the shared experience of opposition to unionism and the late development of a substantial Catholic middle class. Few of the Catholic grammar schools, even today, have any of the burnished social confidence visible in the pillars of the Protestant system.

The IRA and Sinn Féin leadership drew its membership disproportionately from the secondary schools, not the Catholic grammars, teacher training colleges and universities. Sinn Féin's minister for education, Martin McGuinness, has made much of his own relegation to a secondary school by the eleven-plus examination; he deems it inhuman and has overtly set out to replace the selection system. The effort has already begun to be bogged down in opposition from the grammar schools lobby, both Protestant and Catholic, and from unionist politicians, many of them former pupils of the biggest and longest-established grammars. Much of the political pro-grammar schools lobby is motivated by dislike of the Sinn Féin minister, side by side with possessive pride in a system that was once a bulwark of the ruling unionist establishment. Protestant feeling that education has only delivered for a selfish and largely unpolitical middle class is incoherent and almost unvoiced.

Debate on selection and integration is fought out on muddy ground. In defence of separation, and selection, there is much that is difficult if not impossible to articulate, and as much that cannot be avowed. Donal Flanagan of CCMS is an outgoing, charming spokesman who can speak for hours without notes, persuasive about the place of Catholic schools in the community and the historic centrality of the school system. He has more difficulty in isolating the specifically Catholic element in such an atmosphere. 'If I see nothing to distinguish the school from a controlled school, I say you have no right to call yourself a Catholic school. I want to see a mission statement in print, with the central aim to develop each child. Then in the classroom, I want to hear Good morning Mr Flanagan, see children holding the door, children who are happy.' And what in that is distinctly Catholic? 'It's not always easy to articulate but it is manifest; if you visit different schools it is visible.'

His dissection of support for integration echoes that of others in the Catholic education system:

> I see a number of groups who choose to send their children to integrated schools: people who are deeply committed to the notion of greater participation between communities, and are prepared to exercise that commitment by sending their children to integrated schools, and I have nothing but the utmost respect for them. There is a group for whom the decision in relation to a school is very difficult because of their marital circumstances, mixed marriages, and I respect that. I would like to see that they had a more philosophical commitment than just a sort of practical approach. Then there is a group which just wants to run their own schools, and that is a very dangerous thing: a group of people who have no will to be part of the wider community, and are very forceful in terms of what it is that they want their child to be taught.
>
> There is a group of parents who would choose an integrated school in terms of an opt-out, and the best example I could find of that is in Derry, where the intake of the integrated post-primary would draw a lot of male pupils from Catholic families but wouldn't do so in relation to females. In other words some parents say, 'I'm quite happy for my daughter to go to a maintained school because it's very good whereas to send my son, particularly if he's a sensitive sort of individual, into an all-boys' school, that's something I will not countenance. If you're talking about people who are philosophically committed to integrated education … ? Their commitment is to their children, which again I understand.

The belated compliment on commitment rang slightly hollow, coming as it did after a generally unsympathetic interpretation of what motivates integrated parents. Commitment to children's welfare, while beyond criticism, clearly could not measure up to a 'philosophy', however articulated.

> People talk about integrated education being the way forward, it's going to change the world that we live in. If that's so, presumably you have to have a cohort of people who share that. What I'm saying to you is that not all parents who send their children to integrated schools show a philosophical commitment to integrated education. It's because they don't want them to go to some other school. It's an easy option. In some cases we get the propaganda that integrated education is growing and growing. I'm saying we need to examine why it is that parents send their children to integrated schools. I'd almost say, and I don't have any evidence to support this, for the majority it's not that they're totally committed to the philosophy of integrated education. If we built another set of schools and called them the Flanagan schools, because they're new, attracting new staff and new principals, they'd attract pupils.
>
> Also, in terms of we're now twenty years into integrated education, I'm beginning to wonder what impact it has actually made in relation to attitudes. Recently I was conscious of the fact that in north Belfast two groups of children left a school in the afternoon only to be on the streets at night-time hurling stones and rocks at each other. We have a very divided society in north Belfast. But if I was the principal of that school, I would at least have a hope that the children in my school would not be involved in that. So I question what contribution has integrated education made in hard terms.

This was a fairly startling assertion, that because some pupils at one integrated school cheerfully admitted taking part in sectarian rioting, the contribution of integrated education could be questioned. It came particularly oddly from a spokesman for a sector that has educated the overwhelming majority of republicans, responsible for the deaths of nearly 1,800 people during the Troubles. But Donal Flanagan rejected the comparison, though his rejection ran on into a useful admission of underlying resentment.

'There are arguments and counter arguments on all of this, and obviously when children leave school that's where the influence the school has on their lives diminishes very quickly. Put the evidence in the wider context. In terms of philosophy, the aims of the integrated sector, they've set themselves up to bring people together.' Pressed a little more, he showed steadily diminishing attachment to his original proposition: 'It's foolish of teachers to think they can change the world. The comment didn't come from me, it came from a teacher in an integrated school. I'm not going to set myself up as a judge.'

Integrated education brings out a disposition to question, a degree of dislike, even open opposition among people who would never dream of questioning, much less disparaging, any other area of someone else's life. Among those who are professional educators, or involved in education administration, the questioning tends to be sharper, the opposition more blatant. Clearly, the integrated schools lobby galls the other sectors by suggesting superior motivation.

It rarely seems to occur to questioners that they might be revealing more of their own philosophy or attitudes than they intend. Few would consciously aim, surely, to belittle any couple, mixed or not, who decided they would prefer their child to attend a school established to value equally children of both those denominations, children of other faiths and none, in a context that treated both the dominant cultures in Northern Ireland with equal respect. Yet that is what the questioning often does, by implicitly or explicitly attributing less good, less serious, more selfish or more superficial motives to parents who decide against the separate systems.

Choose an integrated school for your children in many places, for whatever mixture of reasons, and you make a public statement that many dislike. One of the most ill-judged criticisms there has ever been of integrated schools is that they are a sop to idle consciences removed from the real world. There is nothing removed, for example, about the Hazelwood schools, secondary and primary, slap in the middle of a north Belfast interface where rioting in the first two years of the new century seethed back and forth for months at a stretch – the teenage rioters Donal Flanagan referred to attended Hazelwood College.

'You made him too trusting,' one Hazelwood teacher was told when a former pupil, a Catholic, was shot and killed at his mainly Protestant workplace in January 2002.

When schools became a north Belfast front line, much of the surrounding discussion hinged on the fairly unthinking assertion that if only one school system existed, 'this' would never have happened – meaning the behaviour that started with aggressive loyalist picketing at the Catholic Holy Cross Primary School, and widened for a time into attacks on other schools. Few of those who made the assertion could seriously have meant that because Catholics were being attacked by Protestants, this meant Catholic schools should close and Catholic children should attend what are in effect Protestant schools. A muddy quality in some comments did suggest, however, that a lingering and basic misapprehension is widely held. The only thing that prevents Protestant schools from being truly integrated, this runs, is the inexplicable, stubborn and possibly bad-minded refusal of Catholics to abandon their separate sector.

A growing number of Catholics choose schools where pupils process daily past flags and emblems of Britishness and meet on ceremonial occasions for assemblies led in prayer by ministers ordained in some Protestant denomination, concluded by the British national anthem. Most, if not all, of these schools make little effort to reflect the cultural background, religious or political outlook of their offspring: they are unselfconsciously, and in some cases markedly, British and Protestant in ethos, staff and school customs often reflecting an unthinking, unquestioning unionist outlook. The norm is Protestant: Catholic students might be welcome but need not expect to see their community reflected in the school's everyday life. Yet newly rich and confident, and relaxed about political and religious identity, these Catholics send their children to a string of major grammar schools. They worked for Protestants for decades, the thinking appears to be, so why not for us? Observers of the new political balance, or imbalance, between despondent unionism and assertive nationalism see the trend as yet another example of a willingness to reverse traditional communal behaviour. 'They've begun to take over the housing in affluent Protestant places, so why wouldn't they move in on their good schools?' one analyst questions. 'What do you bet they'll change those to suit themselves too?'

The latest wave of Catholics to choose the prestigious and de facto Protestant schools for their children is considerable, recent statistics suggest. 'I liked the look of Stranmillis,' one Catholic explains, naming a controlled primary school not far from Queen's University in pleasant leafy south Belfast. 'A good mix, a good school, other nationalities there too.' It followed that she would send her children next to Methody, rather than to Lagan, though she was too polite to explain precisely why Methody was preferable. 'For my husband and myself it was simply a question of trying to make sure the children didn't grow up like us, knowing only Catholics at school.' The unspoken explanation for choosing the state option rather than integration seemed to be proven social and academic desirability.

Jan O'Neill, who helped start North Coast, a secondary integrated school in Coleraine, County Londonderry, and who was also involved in Mill Strand Primary nearby, says this approach once annoyed her but she has become more tolerant. 'When I started I was a purist. Now I can see that though this seems far from perfect there's more than one way to achieve your aims. At the start you might see nothing but the purest way.' It is an attitude that the Catholic Church is arguably displaying towards parents in affluent south Belfast, who in the church's terms are nonconformist. For several years now a number of parents have run their own confession, communion and confirmation preparation class for children who do not attend the local Catholic schools, but are pupils at Stranmillis, and at the various preparatory departments of local Protestant grammars. The class is held in an annexe of St Bride's primary school, and is advertised in the parish newsletter. 'It's gone on now through a change or two of parish priest. Some clearly hardly think about it, one more or less held his nose and pretended not to notice. People asked for it and the answer was yes,' says a devout and conformist parishioner who wholly approves.

For those who started the integrated movement thirty years ago by running just such classes for their children, and as a consequence, were refused confirmation for the children by the bishop, this must seem a quite remarkable shift. Many parish priests still treat as impertinence the suggestion that although Catholic teachers with the Church's certification have prepared them for the sacraments, children in integrated schools should take First Communion with the other children in their parishes, on the same day and in the same ceremony. The message is that the Church should not be asked to recognise another system, since Catholic schools exist. Successive bishops have refused all requests from integrated schools for chaplains.

Even while they deplore the insensitivity to children and their parents, some in integrated education would admit there is a logic to this official Church position. But the class in the St Bride's annexe means that Catholics in affluent south Belfast, who send their children to Protestant rather than integrated schools, are welcomed inside a Catholic school, enabled to advertise their class in a Church publication, and are effectively being assisted by the Church to make good the deficiency, as the Church sees it, in their children's religious training caused by their own decision not to choose a Catholic school. They are being helped to have their cake and eat it, not an assistance offered elsewhere. The cynical might see it as an example of the Church's famed ability to swim with new tides, and to handle the same matter in different ways depending on the status, religious or social, of the supplicants.

The Catholic Church rolls with the punches in one of its most upmarket stations, judging the weight of opinion to be critical and worth handling in sympathetic fashion, a supple judgement characteristic of a long-lived institution. Will a critical mass of Catholic enrolment in time transform other institutions? The effects are not yet clear and will be fascinating to study. Two of Belfast's best-known schools, Methody and Belfast Royal Academy, now have sizeable Catholic contingents. In south and north Belfast respectively, these schools have been faced with comparatively rapid and far-reaching demographic and political changes. Observers wait to see if in response their staffs become proportionately Catholic.

Neither school makes public comment on balance in their enrolment. In rapidly changing north Belfast, where Protestant flight began with the middle class but is now comprehensive, the principals of some feeder primary schools estimate that enrolment in Belfast Royal Academy might now be almost one-third Catholic, with staff balance beginning to reflect that. Parents and teachers suggest that the school has made little or no real adjustment: 'the pitch is to describe it as non-denominational or multi-denominational, and that's that,' says a staff member.

Presentation may have become a little more sophisticated since 1987, when the headmaster of another prestigious Belfast school blithely contributed his thoughts to a unionist Belfast paper, the *News Letter*, on integrated education. The principal of the Royal Belfast Academical Institution (known as 'Inst'), Thomas Garrett, said of the venerable boys' school, 'Inst lives in the shadow of Divis Flats and the school has always had a liberal tradition. We are not concerned about the location of Divis at the moment. We do absorb children from liberal Roman Catholic parents. These parents want to send their children to a non-denominational, non-sectarian school that has always prided itself on a liberal schooling. We are delighted to see Roman Catholic children coming to Inst, but at the moment we cannot see substantial numbers of children coming from republican areas, because they are already well catered for at their own denominational schools, for example on the Falls Road.'

The drill for major institutions today, it appears, is to say little or nothing about school policy and do little or nothing to change school ethos as its student make-up changes. But when possible, the tags non-denominational/mixed/cross-community are invoked. In recent years Methody's student body has become 25 per cent Catholic, according to staff a steadily expanding component, many at sixth form but also in lower forms such as first form. The school is proud of the shift, but shows little interest in reflecting it formally. In the ceremonies beloved of a highly self-conscious and formal institution there will be no declared transformation, it seems. Nor will there be attempts to recruit more Catholic teachers and so provide pupils with staff mixed in similar proportions to enrolment. 'Not our way,' says one insider. 'Evolution's our preferred route.' Catholic teachers? 'There are a number. I've really no idea how many.' It should be remembered, it was pointed out, that while the school had always been proud to call itself inter-denominational, with Muslim pupils from Malaysia and else-where, it was obliged by the terms of its foundation to retain close links with Methodism. So there was little or no likelihood of opting for transformation. 'We emphasise cross-community development as much as we can, we cultivate links with Catholic schools. If Catholic parents want their children to take time off on holy days, there's never been any trouble about that. I don't think there's the slightest sign of any groundswell of dissatisfaction with our style.' Clearly, this is true. The growing numbers of Catholic pupils are evidence that many middle-class Catholic parents are perfectly happy with Methody's laid-back approach towards their sizeable and steadily expanding minority.

By contrast, a founder parent who has also been a teacher in a school with low numbers of Catholics, but with pretensions none-theless to being mixed, even 'integrated,' fumes at what he terms the 'smugness' that sees no need to adjust ethos when the pupil body changes. 'Ask them how they respect the identity of the Catholic pupils they've got, and they'll look at you. Ask have they plans to teach Irish and introduce gaelic games, what newspapers they have each day in the school library, are they ready to change school holidays to cater for Catholic holy days, do they invite the Irish universities to visit as well as the British ... or are they doing any of these things already? Silence.'

By virtue of having had several children already at school before integrated schools were founded, and two more later, another founder parent has experience of both kinds: of integrated schools and also of several big-name institutions which pride themselves on their 'non-denominational, mixed' intake. 'There's no comparison.

In one kind if you're the minority you're tolerated, or invisible. I remember my fella, one of his friends saying to him when they went off to a formal with his school, a very posh one, "don't tell the world you're a Catholic". I retold this story in front of a much-respected headmaster of another major grammar school and he nearly fell over, he turned white with rage. "Are you implying that one of our finest schools is sectarian?" he said.'

Some awareness of the need to show flexibility was perhaps visible in Methody's atypical welcome for Sinn Féin's minister of education, Martin McGuinness, early in his term of office, while antirepublican pupil walk-outs from other schools were still taking place. Early in 2002, a question in the Stormont Assembly established that, after a full year in the job, Mr McGuinness had received invitations from only eleven schools that were clearly not Catholic. Perhaps Methody's invitation had more significance than a pragmatic intent to adjust to a new political era.

At bottom, the most damaging reaction to integrated education might be the least sectional and partisan. 'They think they're better than the rest of us,' says a determinedly nonsectarian and fair-minded parent of now adult children, a partner in a mixed marriage who has thought long and hard about prejudice in its various forms in Northern Ireland, for work purposes as well as in pursuit of being a decent citizen. 'People who choose integrated schools sometimes give me the impression that they think it's a badge of superiority. They chose the right schools, so their politics and everything else must be above board. And the rest of us by implication choose the wrong schools. I must admit, I don't like that. It gets my back up.'

This was a parent who, as part of a mixed marriage, had agreed to a Catholic primary school because the religious, 'believing', partner was Catholic. At secondary level, the couple chose Methody because they saw it as academically good, high-status in terms of what it would do for their children's career prospects, and 'mixed' in their terms, having a growing proportion of Catholic pupils. They did not see it as in any way inferior to a consciously mixed school, designated from the outset as integrated.

They are proud that their children have grown up to fit neatly into neither major group, that they will in fact be able to say truthfully when asked to tick official boxes, that they are neither Irish nor British, neither Protestant nor Catholic, but 'Other'. But this couple do not like what they take to be the self-righteousness of a pro-integrated education community. It is not an uncommon attitude, and deserves examination. The irony is that it assumes the existence of a community, where there is at best in many eyes a ramshackle coincidence of motivation, and an assortment of political and religious stances.

Hostility in this case is the result of a mistaken impression, of confusing occasional statements by individuals speaking for integrated education with the views of a 'movement' which does not exist as an organised entity. Some enemies are earned, even necessary. A quantity of hostility may be the price to be paid for challenging unthinking assumptions, for disturbing the smugness of people who elevate slipshod thinking to the status of philosophy purely by invoking the name and reputation of an ancient religion. But can integrated education afford to alienate those who should be well-disposed, who themselves turn away from the easy solidarity and unearned belonging conferred by blocs, and who question traditional patterns of schooling?

Where does the image of self-righteousness come from, and can it be dispelled? A parent whose children are now at an integrated secondary, and who came through an integrated primary, says she has often found herself 'turned off' by the tone she hears from supporters of the sector and from other parents. 'I think all of us, including myself, are a bit self-righteous. We're inclined to maybe forgive ourselves for other attitudes because we feel we're on the moral high ground just by choosing these schools. As if that proves what good people we are, completely free of bigotry.'

In her experience this is not true of a considerable number of parents, and she again included herself. 'There's a lot of refusing to think beyond the obvious. Leave the kids at the school and that's your duty done.' For someone originally Protestant in upbringing, who had lived for years outside Northern Ireland and hoped that the 'integrated world' would offer an island of radical, nonsectarian thought, there was some disillusion involved in her choice of schools for her children. 'It would be good for us all to be shaken up and have to think again. The assumption is that we don't have to do any work on ourselves because we're just perfect, we're integrated, that's the end of the story.'

In another version of this attitude, selling the idea of integrated education sounded to some ears like 'another sort of evangelism, no more attractive to me than the wilder shores of Ian Paisley really. There's enough people in Northern Ireland who think they have the answer, if everyone would just shut up and go along with them.' These were people who supported the schools, and who would keep their children there. Nor was their choice of school shaped by any of the arguments so often used by enemies to denigrate integrated education. Two of the children involved were academic high-flyers and high achievers by any standards, all of them had considerable social skills, and the parents were keen on having them taught in a social mix. The integrated schools they attended could not be described as middle-class enclaves, even by the most stubborn enemy, if truthful about enrolment and location.

The accusation that integration is a snobbish choice is the most stubborn of the accusations, in part because it is true of a section of parents who profess to choose a mixed school for religious and cultural reasons, but who in reality are in flight from the selection procedure's determination that their child should go to a tough, working-class secondary school. Many of those who make the accusation will themselves have avoided sending a child to a secondary, but they see no contradiction in using the charge against others.

The offence of the integrated sector, in many minds, is that by its existence it indicts the other two sectors for maintaining sectarian division, if not for actively adding to it. By implication these are more high-minded parents, and those in the other sectors, unsurprisingly, will not have it. The accusation of elevating snobbery to the status of philosophy is an efficient form of ridicule. There is a conviction that integrated education must be denied any claim to superiority.

Pressing a claim to virtue on behalf of a project is not the same as boasting of personal virtue, and public supporters of integrated education are wise to make it plain that they know the difference. Perhaps the best that can be done is to be honest about the mixture of motives among parents, and to be vigilant about the tone of public statements. Some of the most sweeping claims for integrated education tend to come from people who know little about Northern Ireland. The sector might usefully discuss the subject with well-wishers.

4
Teachers and Schools

In the early days, some teachers took considerable risks when they joined an integrated school. Once, Catholic teachers feared that they would never work again in the maintained sector after joining an integrated school. Initially, a number had doubts about the chances of these new schools surviving. Those who came from the controlled sector in particular talk about the mockery from colleagues: 'I remember being called the Mickey Mouse Greenham Common Left,' says one. Yet Sheila Greenfield, the first integrated headteacher and, as she points out, also the first woman appointed head of a coeducational school in Northern Ireland, recalls fondly how, against the mood of the time, a couple of principals welcomed her to the club of head teachers. 'The principals of Methody and Grosvenor treated me as a fellow professional. I don't know what they really thought,' she laughs, 'but they behaved as though "We're a school, and you're a school." Starting out in a hut, that mattered very much.'

With only a few years spent teaching in Belfast, most of her experience having been in big English comprehensives, the last of which had a multicultural enrolment, Sheila Greenfield was in extra need of friendship and solidarity in a strange land. Integrated schools remained strange new territory for most of the pioneers, and for more onlookers, for some considerable time. It is a measure of progress that some now think a spell in 'integration' looks good on a c.v. and teachers say that movement between the sectors is far from uncommon. Yet to many minds, there is still a considerable difference in atmosphere between integrated schools and 'the mainstream', and between the attitudes of teachers inside the different sectors.

'It's almost tangibly different,' says an academic with connections to the sector that date almost to the beginning. 'Granted, one school day's routine can be much the same anywhere – but there is a buzz, an excitement, about integrated schools which never fails to impress me.' This is not a description that fits all the schools, according to teachers in a considerable number, and slightly saddened practitioners and observers in others. 'One or two have lost their edge,' a somewhat disillusioned well-wisher remarks. 'There are new staff coming in who think of it mainly as a career option,' says a veteran with experience of both the integrated and maintained sectors, clearly half-amused and half-concerned at a shift that would have seemed unthinkable in the early years. 'They're mildly interested in integration, that's all. Grand kids, good teachers too, some of them – but being integrated's a bit of an afterthought.'

A more frequent visitor than the still-impressed academic, described bringing a close relative, who had long experience at senior levels in various controlled schools, to several integrated schools in succession. 'She wasn't enthusiastic in advance,' he says. 'But when we came away she said, "Everyone we met was almost too good to be true, but it was real. This child-centred stuff – they genuinely sounded caring."' Were controlled schools not child-centred and caring too, he asked? '"We-ell," she said, "you can't put your finger on it but no, they're not, not to the same extent."'

She was particularly struck by one member of staff in a small integrated primary school, whose responsibilities were listed in the school's prospectus to demonstrate how all staff took pride in their contributions. ' "He can't do all this," she said, "this is a wind-up." Yet within five minutes of meeting the guy it was clear it was all correct, and he did more than that. He was on the board of governors, he was a founding parent, he was working on the plans for the new school, he organises the football, he goes on all the trips and he's the caretaker.' That was in Enniskillen, where the multi-tasking Charlie McAuley got involved in the mourning aftermath of the 1987 bombing with the inspirational local organiser John Maxwell, part of whose own commitment was a form of tribute to his fifteen-year-old son Paul, killed in the 1979 IRA bombing on board Lord Mountbatten's boat.

Local factors have helped to shape many of the schools, as they do in the other sectors though perhaps less vividly and directly. Many would say that the personalities of founder parents and teachers are also influential for years, though there is considerable variety in the relationships between integrated staff and principals. Some aim for an idealised and collegial approach, others are comparatively traditional and disciplinarian. 'We're all on the same learning curve,' said one particularly enthusiastic principal. Another says, 'We can hardly set out to integrate pupils if we aren't working on ourselves.'

Put several teachers together, however, ask how integrated schools resemble each other and how they differ, and it is clear that atmosphere varies as much as do interpretations of integration. 'They run a tight ship,' said a wide-eyed teacher about the nearest integrated neighbour. 'It's meetings meetings all the way. We've got someone from it lately and she can't believe the relaxed atmosphere here. She thought maybe all integrated schools were uptight.'

Staff of integrated schools, unsurprisingly, are as varied as the parents who choose them or who first opened them. 'Integrated' teachers include evangelists, the serious-minded and thoughtful, cheerful but undoctrinaire enthusiasts, some clear-eyed careerists, a large number who are committed in a rather vague way, perhaps even a few cynics. Some teachers might spend no more time thinking about the purpose of the schools they work in than the overworked staff of any number of mainstream schools. There are also a number, as in any other school, who put in their day with as little self-examination as possible.

Others try to spark debates in the staff room and yearn for more time to talk to colleagues about identity and how to handle contentious issues with pupils. A number are clearly thinking hard about the need to 'revise thinking' in the light of 'the Good Friday Agreement', the 'new mood since the ceasefires', the sense of equal opportunity and risk in the wake of the Burns Report on the organisation of education at second level and the debate it sparked on replacing selective education. A wide cross-section have been concerned for some time about 'governance', the high wastage rate of principals, and the need for a coordinating, more authoritative central body than NICIE. By contrast, one principal expresses considerable impatience with talk of theorising about the purpose of the schools. 'We need clarification of the role of governors, all right. For me, integrated education is very simple. It's about improving community relations, healing divisions, and democracy in a deeply divided society. It's not about parent power, or teachers' powers.'

Though many talk about lack of coherence, and the need for a statutory central body, some personalities and their views are widely known and instantly identifiable. Was it a widely held view that integration was about 'improving community relations', not about parent power? 'Ah, that'll be Y,' said a series of other principals, one after the other. 'I know who you're talking about. Too aggressive.' One said drily, 'Y likes a good confrontation.' Another asked, 'But you've heard Y's problems with parents and governors?'

Political views among integrated teachers, according to observers and supporters alike, are more mixed than some might suppose. Their ranks include a number of Orangemen, on the staffs of 'greenfield' schools as well as, more predictably, teaching in the 'transformed', former controlled schools. This surprises some pupils and a number of parents, who question – but as far as can be established only in private conversation and not in the form of complaint to schools – whether members of an avowedly anti-Catholic organisation can show the tolerance surely essential to integration. 'It's a process,' says a senior teacher. 'We're none of us integrated. We're all *integrating*, if we're anything: we haven't finished this business, how could we have? Orangemen in a school that's going about its business the right way will be changing themselves all the time, just by being there.'

Others argue, sometimes fiercely, that the ideal will be reached only when the entire range of political opinion is present routinely in integrated schools. One teacher became uncharacteristically angry at the very idea that an Orangeman might be out of place. 'Why shouldn't we have the extremes as well as the self-consciously moderate and liberal? Isn't that what we should really be about?'

The range of religious beliefs among staff include Christian fundamentalism and denial of evolution. There are also a considerable number who make no secret of their preference for secular schools as the ideal. These tend to be teachers in schools whose governors and principals from the start regretted what some call the 'heavy emphasis on Christianity' as a central tenet of integration. A number would be much happier if integrated schools in Northern Ireland did not lay such emphasis on religion. As well as the secularists, they include some of the most fundamentalist, who think that religion should be taught at home by committed Christian parents.

In schools that have 'transformed', it seems probable that at least a few teachers are opposed to integration and remain on the staff out of sheer doggedness, or because they are afraid they may not find work elsewhere. Others maintain that these teachers too might change in time, given a commitment by governors and senior management to a process of genuine transformation (see Chapter 6), and the necessary vigilance by government in the shape of DENI.

LOCATION

Part of the distinctiveness of many integrated schools is of course in their surroundings, the odd buildings that have housed a considerable number, and the makeshift style of their first and perhaps formative years. A number of teachers think those experiences have helped shape a school spirit and wonder if it will survive new, custom-built premises. Others see the changes already diminishing what they had come to think of as a special quality, but which they now speculate might have been no more than determination in adversity. As what some call the 'foundation phase' passes, some in the tribe of scholarly observers who have charted every minute of the integrated school story can also see risks for individual schools, and for the sector.

Grace Fraser has written and co-written a number of detailed studies, and has also been a school governor. She says adjusting to being under observation is a factor. 'A problem for integrated schools which has never been resolved is how to come to terms with external perceptions of them. This is why when Valerie Morgan and I wrote our last research report we called it *In the Frame* [Coleraine: University of Ulster, 1999]. That seemed appropriate because it works both ways, in that the schools are now numerous enough to make an impact but also have to share what goes with becoming established. Part of the fear is of course that the longer they are established, the more they are in danger of becoming ordinary, that is, just like the rest.'

Among those who have the most experience of integrated schools, and have also spent time in controlled or maintained teaching, there is a strong echo of Grace Fraser's theme. 'I see young teachers coming into this now as a career option,' said one veteran with a touch of melancholy. 'I listen to my young colleagues and sometimes I think it's becoming like Catholic schools – where you go for an interview and you're asked "Are you willing to teach religion?" You know to say "Oh yes, I'd love to!" But you're thinking, "Fingers crossed, hope it doesn't happen." The same thing's happening here. "Oh yes, I'm very committed to integration." They might get to be, but it isn't something they've thought about at all. It's just a job.'

Insisting that the difference between integrated and other schools remains considerable, if difficult to measure, Grace Fraser vividly recalls the look of integrated education at its most distinctive. 'Most early schools were a devil to find. I always had to allow an extra half an hour before an interview for touring around the outskirts of towns, stopping to ask the locals who had almost always never heard of the school, far less "integrated" anything. They rarely looked like schools – classrooms in factory buildings, church halls, old folks' homes, former wings of psychiatric hospitals, mobile cities in the mud – but when you went in, you knew you were somewhere very special.'

Among the oddest of school settings, the secondary schools of Drumragh and Oakgrove stand out. Drumragh has functioned for seven years in the old Omagh asylum. Oakgrove is for the most part a 'city in the mud' of forty-seven mobile classrooms, its one proper building the old 'Gransha', Derry's former mental hospital, whose name for decades has been synonymous with depression and the sadness of crushing despair, as in 'It'd put you in Gransha'. But Oakgrove is thriving; it is among the largest of the integrated colleges and is proud to have become a serious player among locally famous schools like Thornhill, St Columb's, and Foyle and Londonderry College.

Walking through Drumragh's high corridors and narrow stone stairways with principal Kathleen Hinds, on the day she wrote her retirement letter, it was plain that thanks to staff determination and ingenuity the old hospital setting had lent spirit to the Omagh school, rather than depressing it. The quiet buzz of classes came from long high-ceilinged rooms, once closed wards. 'We thought we'd be here for six months at most, and it's six years later,' Kathleen Hinds said. 'A huge wooden chair in the hallway, with straps and a hole in the middle of the seat.' She shudders at the memory. 'For the first spell, we were sharing the building. There were psychiatrists still seeing patients in one section. We heard we were described as the cuckoo in the nest, but we've grown, and we pushed them out.' She was leaving proud in the knowledge that her granddaughter would be starting as a new Year Eight the following September. Whereas in 1995 the new Drumragh faced the leftovers of Victorian psychiatry, a now-thriving school has a grand new building on the stocks, approved in March 2002 by Martin McGuinness.

A young teacher said Drumragh was his first coeducational experience after an all-boys primary and secondary, and male teacher training college. 'It's nearly as big a thing for me as the integration bit, but then aren't we supposed to be integrating across the board.' In Omagh, few conversations with outsiders go far before stumbling over the agonising aftermath of the 1998 bombing by the anti-peace process Real IRA, which killed twenty-nine people and left many others with injuries that will need years of treatment and many that are untreatable. 'The town's still a disaster zone,' said the young teacher. 'There's wounds that'll never heal. I think like all the schools in Omagh, we know we have to give the kids even more than other places.'

Kathleen Hinds described being asked to allow the Drumragh building to be used for the inquests on the bombing fatalities and regretfully refusing. It had been hard enough to establish a school identity in the hospital, she thought: children needed a space to learn, some distance from tragedy. A local member of staff remarked on how much of Omagh is rigidly segregated, a mood this person saw developing as the peace process repeatedly stumbled through political obstruction. 'When the fighting stops, are we just going to go for the lowest common denominator? Keep the heads down and not talk about it? We have kids here together from the estates at the two ends of the town. It can be tight enough.'

But integration was 'a joke' if sharp issues were not openly tackled. 'You get the odd graffiti in the boys' toilets: the one I liked best was *The only reason I'm here is my ma sent me*. A boy said kind of proudly in a discussion the other day, "no I don't have any Catholic friends" and some took him up on it. But they managed to keep the conversation going well enough.' The teacher was cheered that the boy with no Catholic friends left the classroom for break-time 'with a crowd that was right and mixed'.

Integrating education clearly calls for different approaches in different places, schools taking on the socio-economic coloration of catchment areas and at times some of the political mood of their surroundings, if only as reaction to it. Omagh's Drumragh is very different in appearance to Brownlow in Craigavon, a striking new sign outside announcing BROWNLOW INTEGRATED COLLEGE, though the endless confusing roundabouts of Craigavon still are decorated with more than one ageing road sign directing the unwary to BROWNLOW HIGH SCHOOL. It is now the only trans-forming integrated school that others in the integrated sector recognise, many with real warmth, as having made a sustained and impressive effort to widen its appeal and grow beyond its original, largely monocultural status.

The common thread between Brownlow and Drumragh is their effort to reflect and be part of the community around them. Drumragh perches on the edge of Omagh, waiting with hope to move into a new complex and a new phase of existence, after difficult years in a town full of suffering. Brownlow sees itself creating a new school identity in a place that notoriously lacks any sense of itself as an established and unified community. Teachers who have been there from the start, plus a wave of enthusiastic newcomers, firmly believe that integrating a school feeds into a wider communal process.

Craigavon has many spirited people but a dispirited history. It was built in the sixties by a unionist government to be Northern Ireland's third city and a magnet for industrial development, deliberately sited near strongly Protestant Portadown and named after the founding father of the unionist state, as nationalists com-plained. The plan went adrift as old industries failed, newly arrived plants proved short-lived, Portadown and Lurgan declined to become part of a linear city, and the troubles flared. A belt of housing between the two towns, linked by one roundabout after another, was named Brownlow. The high school, built as a con-trolled school, which hoped it might genuinely draw a mixed enrolment, always had some Catholic staff but was mainly Protestant; it looked out at uprooted fields and raw concrete.

When the big anchor firm of Goodyear folded at the start of the eighties, economic migrants from Belfast and elsewhere became the new unemployed in estates that varied between the well planned

and the shoddy. Craigavon 'centre', near the school, was for decades
a windy, empty bad joke. A high incidence of mixed marriage
between Protestants and Catholics and of people who refuse to be
defined as either, a sizeable Chinese community, even briefly a
group of Vietnamese 'boat people', formed the nucleus of a richer
mix of races and classes than in any other area of the same size in
Northern Ireland. But the strip of land between Portadown and
Lurgan, which the optimists hoped would become the heart of the
new city, never outgrew its origins as Brownlow, a string of estates
which in time became a byword for drug abuse, petty crime, and
family breakdown. In many minds, this is a difficult place in which
to live, never mind transform a school.

The long slow transition of the school from failing controlled
secondary towards a new life as an integrated school came in the
teeth of bitter opposition. Madge Steel, the first woman shop
steward in Goodyear and an early campaigner to transform the
Brownlow school, remembers a couple of women opponents
collecting signatures door to door. She refused to sign. 'You'll send
your kids to a Fenian hole?' one woman asked her incredulously.
'We'll lose our Protestant school,' they told her. She says now, 'I
said my children loved it and so they did, and their children love it
too: it's a part of my life.'

It took ballot after ballot of parents to secure Brownlow's transformation, as local DUP and Ulster Unionist councillors continually
attacked it. Although the area around the school steadily became
more Catholic and in parts republican in sympathy, not surprisingly Catholic parents were slow to send their children to it. Yearly
confrontations outside nearby Portadown over the Orange Order's
determination to march from the church at Drumcree through the
Catholic Garvaghy Road have heightened tensions in the entire
area. 'Brownlow survived Drumcree,' says one admiring supporter.
'That's no mean feat.' But it has taken ten years to achieve 30 per
cent Catholic enrolment, and to reach the point where seven out of
a teaching staff of twenty-six are also Catholic.

Madge Steele, in declining health and in her late seventies, still
goes in to tutor teenagers with writing and reading difficulties, and

has helped young teachers through an 'anti-conflict' strategy. A major part of the strategy seems to have been 'granny power', big young men deferring to a small woman with a formidable sense of humour, kindness, and a quick tongue. A younger woman, June White, who campaigned originally for the transformation, has run a five-year pilot peer mediation scheme, as recommended in the Department of Education's guidelines on transformation.

The school has worked hard to erase old perceptions and create a new image. A fleet of local buses in 2001 carried large advertisements congratulating Brownlow GCSE pupils on their results. After a long spell in another school that has often caught media interest, the successful and huge Falls Road girls' comprehensive St Louise's, Brian O'Kelly was recruited to Brownlow as 'Vice-Principal – Integration'. He had worked in St Louise's with a pioneer in community education, Pauline Murphy, bringing adults into the school to learn, take courses and eventually examinations alongside children. Helping to transform a school in a place that is also being regenerated is a logical development of his previous job, he thinks.

FLAGS, NAMES AND OTHER PROBLEMS

In the old and tiny city on the banks of the Foyle, which saw the plan to build Craigavon as an affront to its own status, one of the first questions for the founders of integrated schools was what to call the place they live in: Derry, or Londonderry? The group of parents who became the Foyle Trust for Integrated Education have now known each other for several years, long enough for some at least to feel comfortable talking about the basic divisions in Northern Ireland, and for a measure of mutual trust to develop. A Catholic member of the group recalls holding a meeting at an early stage, on a night when the then Irish president Mary Robinson visited the city's Guildhall for a conference. 'We went for a drink and we were talking about the visit, and this person, a strong supporter of the schools, said she didn't think Mary Robinson should have been invited because she was the leader of a hostile state. I was really struck: I admired Mary Robinson a lot. But it was obvious to me this was a real genuine emotion, where if I hadn't known this woman I'd have thought she was just saying it to stick her finger in my eye. I could hear it the way it was meant, because this was a person I trusted.'

Another says that the Derry/Londonderry issue is fundamental, that recognising real sensitivities and finding ways to reflect them must underpin the whole approach to integrated education. 'I say Derry and Londonderry in the same conversation. Those are the wee issues that are important to people. Some would test you to see can they get you to say whatever it is they call it. There are people in this community and it would stick in their craw to say Londonderry.' Though out of the political limelight and off microphones most Protestants unselfconsciously call the place Derry, the name Londonderry has become more than a name and much more than its extra two syllables: for many it seems to have become an endangered relic of the old unionist Northern Ireland.

The two local integrated schools settled on an awkward, patchwork approach. In speech, staff and spokespersons sometimes say one, sometimes the other, and in formal correspondence and on school letterheads they write L'Derry. The principal of Oakgrove Primary, Anne Murray, jokes about it, but says there is no ducking how deep the matter of terminology goes, or how few are truly immune to emotions about it. 'Primary One in the first few days, there was an interesting conversation overheard by a teacher during rest period on the carpet. "Where do you come from?" says one wee girl. "I come from Derry," says another. "You mean Londonderry," says the first. We're talking four years old here.'

Unionists have for years been insisting that they no longer feel welcome or safe in the old centre: Protestants were driven out by IRA bombs and nationalist intimidation, they say. Some accuse nationalists in general and republicans in particular of replacing the old unionist domination with their own triumphalism. In both the primary and secondary integrated schools there is a strong sense of awareness, among teachers and organisers, that Catholics are the huge majority locally, with a corresponding Protestant mix of defensiveness, vulnerability and vigilance against slights. 'When I'm ordering something on the phone for the school I'll say Londonderry in the conversation and I'll also say Derry,' says Anne Murray. 'If someone feels very strongly about it, I'll say what they want.' What the headed notepaper for both schools says, however, is *L'Derry*: integrated education's recognition of which local community is the more angry, dissatisfied and, perhaps, the more vulnerable.

Achieving a balance in numbers has occasionally preoccupied the managers of both the Oakgrove schools. Several Protestant observers with experience of differently balanced areas say that for all the efforts made in the secondary school, 'the Protestants, pupils and teachers, are a bit on the hushed side', as one puts it. 'They feel outnumbered, there's no doubt about it.' There is recognition that 'the wider atmosphere is part of that', but an implication none the less that the school should try harder to counteract it. The most difficult issues for Marie Cowan, the college principal, have been those that involve symbols regarded as embattled talismans: the poppy of Remembrance Day and the black ribbon to commemorate those killed on Bloody Sunday. The latter is a local issue only because it is worn nowhere but Derry, and because Londonderry objects to it so strongly.

'Five years back we had the TV cameras here, a child with a poppy, me saying you have to take it off.' The school's original policy was that the poppy would be officially sold, since it commemorated all the dead of past wars. Then black ribbons appeared which brought strong Protestant protest, and it was decided that no emblems should be worn. Some felt this proposition was 'a cop-out', one teacher said, 'since we're supposed to be open to all and respectful of all. There was a feeling that we must work out a compromise that allowed both emblems in. A lot of us think you're not living in the real world if you ban something.' The compromise proposed was that each emblem be worn to mark Remembrance Day and Bloody Sunday, each for a single day. But a crowded and angry parents' council meeting followed, with the biggest Protestant representation in the school's history, and the 'no emblems' rule began.

There is a lingering dissatisfaction with the outcome. 'The problem wasn't the children,' says Marie Cowan a bit sadly. 'Sometimes people use the children. How can we expect children to work out these things if the adults make such a mess of it?' Similar arguments have raged in other integrated schools: the republican Easter lily pops up occasionally. Schools are instantly nervous about republican symbols, willing on principle to treat the poppy as a nonsectarian and uncontroversial emblem, but in practice they have struggled to bring policy and practice into line. On balance, according to a cross-section of teachers in districts both rural and urban, and in places dominated by each of the two main communities, the bulk of complaints about bruised sensitivities seem to come from Protestants, though there are also Catholic complaints. A teacher west of the Bann, where Catholic school children far outnumber Protestant, and nationalists are in the majority by a considerable margin, looks at the questions for her own school and others in the most Protestant parts of the east. 'The question about culture still has to be addressed properly. What's happening is some schools are looking at Irish, and they're looking at Ulster-Scots, and they see trouble coming. If you offer one and not the other …' Visitors to schools have in general been less contentious, though some are still capable of raising temperatures among parents, if not among pupils.

Mary Robinson's arrival as Irish president in Hazelwood Secondary (Chapter 2) followed years of visits by NIO ministers and occasional royals. Hazelwood has also hosted the Chief Constable of the RUC turned head of the Police Service of Northern Ireland, now retired, Sir Ronnie Flanagan. Catholic parents mollified somewhat by the Robinson visit had grumbled for years among themselves in some schools about the number of visits by British officials and dignitaries. In general, they have been less vocal to principals and boards of governors than their Protestant counterparts, though there are vivid exceptions.

Regular visits by 'community' police officers make few waves, since in spite of occasional republican protests many Catholic schools long ago built them into their routines. But one integrated principal found 'my office door nearly came off the hinges' when the regular community policeman turned up in full riot gear 'just to show the kids apparently what it looked like. Then he meets a republican mother at the door on his way out, so she's straight in to me, fuming.' The follow-up, after soothing the mother, involved 'asking him what he thought he was at – he didn't seem to realise what he'd done'. In another school, where selling poppies had been part of policy from the outset, a mother objected so strongly 'she grabbed me by the throat,' said the principal, 'and threatened to punch me. I explained that we considered the poppy commemorated all the dead of the wars but she wasn't having it. Her father had been interned, wrongly, and she felt very strongly about it. That ended with her taking her children to the convent school up the road.'

Seesaw arguments over emblems test the most tolerant, and the most ingenious. Pressure drives many to black humour: 'If the Pope and the Queen would considerately die on the same day, we could close all the schools no problem,' sighs one weary principal. With increasing focus on Northern Ireland's demographic pattern and the possibility of the Protestant majority coming to an end, segregation has steadily taken on a sharper edge. The 'numbers game' shadows political development, and the lives of many individuals and families living in isolation or massively outnumbered.

For new integrated schools like Ulidia in Carrickfergus, County Antrim, and Strangford, County Down, the surrounding population is predominantly Protestant. There is a similar catchment area for Bangor Central Primary School, and Kircubbin Primary, two County Down schools awarded transformed status in 1998. But for Priory College, Holywood, and Lisburn's Fort Hill College, transformed in the same year, demographic shifts helped prompt the move towards integration. The predominantly Protestant town of Holywood now has a growing Catholic population; strongly Protestant Lisburn, in County Antrim, has an expanding Catholic population only a few miles away in the bulging Belfast suburbs of Poleglass and Twinbrook. Maintaining a balance for the Strangford integrated school means bussing in Catholic pupils from the end of the Ards peninsula where the population becomes slightly more diverse.

Integrated education faces into the post-ceasefires, peace process world with many staff very aware that in the future they will be confronted even more insistently by the baggage of symbolism, and the fundamental question of achieving 'balance'. In buildings erected around them while classes went on, Strangford Integrated College has scarcely had time to draw breath and consider the peace process. Strangford's head of religion, Martin Donaldson, for years a much-respected and popular stalwart of Lagan College, is impatient with the suggestion that classroom teaching is preoccupied with the haggles of the outside world. 'For the adult mind, it's always the same questions: do you teach them about sectarianism, do you tell them about the clashes between Protestants and Catholics? An eleven-year-old doesn't have these perceptions – they're more concerned with somebody having the same fashion sense or supporting the same football team.'

RELIGION DAY-TO-DAY

Martin Donaldson in Strangford says what many others echo, that the day-to-day teaching of religion inside integrated schools has none of the contention and fuss that the question has caused between the schools and the Catholic Church (see Chapter 3). 'We haven't confronted them nearly hard enough,' says one irritated principal. 'There's been too much diplomacy.' A second, equally experienced, and a serious, committed Catholic, thinks 'We've spent far too much time worrying about a Church that's got about six stances towards us.' A third feels inhibited in dealings 'by having to be a polite respectful Protestant' with a bishop who, to all requests for the school's children to receive the sacraments at the same time as Catholic schools, sends 'the same empty letter, hoping I respect his right to think that Catholic schools are the place for Catholic pupils. Never a straight answer: never any answer.'

One sympathetic, knowledgeable and slightly amused onlooker

to the stand-offs between bishops and integrated schools is taken
with the 'realisation, and it seems to have only hit the Church very
recently, that there are more Catholic children in controlled
primaries, and the prep departments of the big voluntary grammars, and the grammars themselves, than there are in integrated
schools. There they are all these years chasing after this paper tiger
of integration.'

It has been quite a chase and often deeply unpleasant. Successive
bishops in the same diocese have taken a different line. The parish
priest in one place can be obstructive, cold, downright hostile and
bad-mannered, while a few miles away another is kind and thoughtful, welcoming to both children and teachers. The document
produced by the bishops early in 2002 spoke fervently of the respect
due to all parents' rights and wishes. Yet the spokesman for the maintained schools, Donal Flanagan, artlessly suggested that most
integrated parents could not expect to have their beliefs taken as
seriously as any Catholic parent, who simply by choosing a Catholic
school demonstrated commitment to a 'philosophy' of education.

Anne Makin has had sharply contrasting experience of dealing
with the Church. She is principal of Saints and Scholars Primary in
Armagh city, where Archbishop Sean Brady has welcomed her
warmly in a gathering of teachers from maintained schools. On his
recommendation, the diocesan schools' religious advisers call to
discuss classes and offer assistance to her teachers. A succession of
specially appointed priests have built up relationships with the
school. It is a story of considerable grace and courtesy from the
Church. Anne Makin's previous experience was very different.

In Newcastle, County Down, as a young teacher of religion in
the All Children's Primary, she watched in horror as her small First
Communion class, all four of them, were taken into a room in the
church by a local Catholic teacher and the parish priest (PP), to be
questioned about their preparedness for the sacraments. She cannot
quite explain now how she was left outside, while the children were
questioned. It sounds as though she was perhaps almost as intimidated as the children. 'They were aged seven and eight. The teacher
did all the questioning, the priest just watched. She was very cold.

They couldn't even say the Hail Mary, she said. I'm still surprised they were able to say anything.' Anne Makin heard later that the children were told it was not surprising they had failed the test, since their teacher was a Protestant. In fact, she is Catholic.

A Newcastle Catholic with connections to the school says that in the parish the intention was clear. 'He was a tough PP, new to the place. I think he thought he'd come down hard on the school and finish them off before they got started. But it backfired badly. People got very angry.' The school had a rocky early history but survived: Anne Makin's class took their test again, with her beside them, and this time were deemed satisfactory.

It is a more dramatic example than most of the churlishness displayed towards integrated schools by a considerable number of priests, and by some teachers in the maintained sector. For many Catholic parents and teachers in integration, the behaviour of the official Church over much of the past twenty years has been a source of considerable pain. 'I think it's a scandal,' says one longtime supporter, a parent governor for several terms. 'It does more harm to the Church than us, it makes them look petty and vindictive.' Like several others, this was someone who had noticed with wry amusement the photograph of children from north Belfast schools together for confirmation in the Holy Cross monastery. The occasion had been organised, and the photographs arranged, to give special place to the children of the Holy Cross school harassed over months by loyalists who often behaved thuggishly. But there also for the occasion, by special request, were Hazelwood Integrated Primary children.

Hazelwood too had experienced the renewed spell of friction on Belfast's streets and sectarian violence that began in 2001: yards from Hazelwood's entrance as tensions flared, Thomas McDonald, a fifteen-year-old Protestant was knocked off his bike by a car and killed in September; former Hazelwood pupil Danny McColgan, a twenty-year-old Catholic, was killed by loyalists in January 2002 as he arrived for work at dawn in strongly Protestant Rathcoole on the city's edge: 'And the bishop who wouldn't confirm Danny McColgan with the rest of his parish, officiated at his funeral,' remarked an integrated teacher with a dismissive toss of the head.

A number of religion teachers inside integrated schools insist that the main issue for them is no longer the preparation of Catholic pupils for the sacraments: many say that it never was, that it merely became convenient media shorthand for integration's relationship with the Catholic Church. Some think there is a new wave of what amounts to clerical benevolence – 'young priests who are well-disposed, some of them aware that it has done the Church no good', as one teacher seasoned in the tussle comments. 'I've heard that several in this diocese are embarrassed. They think it's un-Christian. They can't see what's wrong with us. But most of them would probably prefer to see joint church schools.'

Those in the integrated sector who are most disposed to be understanding about Catholic Church hostility say it is a product of politics and history rather than religion-based, though some still think the original objections were largely coloured by a conviction that the thinking behind integration was predominantly secularist. 'Some in the Catholic Church certainly thought that,' former Lagan principal Brian Lambkin says, 'as did people in the other main churches. Many would still suspect the bulk of integrated parents of being anti-religion.' For him, as for others in the initial founder generation, it was important to show the suspicious that Lagan took religion seriously, and contained committed Christians. The committed Christians were in the majority, or at least they set the predominant tone. By contrast, some involved from early in the movement's history would have preferred entirely secular school-ing. Most of those recognised fairly quickly that it would provide ammunition to many enemies, although not without misgivings which still echo today. A number of later founder parents still regard Lagan as overly conscious of itself as a flagship, and Christian-centred to a degree that they think 'undermines proper integration of all faiths and none', says Jan Kennedy, who has been a parent governor and was a founder of Mill Strand Primary in Portrush, County Antrim. 'That's not what people here wanted.' Lagan principal Helen McHugh defends the school against charges of narrow religiosity by insisting that the two resident chaplains offer the widest form of pastoral care, providing older students in particular with contacts and the opportunity to work in community schemes in deprived urban districts. The school funds the chaplaincy from special collections: a considerable proportion from the tireless Sister Anna's foreign fundraising in latter years. Chaplains over the years have included members of several Protestant churches and Catholic clerical volunteers, the latter implicitly defying the wishes of a series of local bishops.

Clashes with bishops and parish priests about First Communion and confirmation have only served to confirm many supporters of integrated schools in the belief that religion should 'have no place in schools', as one rural parent says. But most parents seem to feel reasonably comfortable in schools which make an effort to be welcoming to all faiths, and none. Jan Kennedy sent her children on to the nearby integrated North Coast College. A determined humanist, she has found integrated education closer to her dreams for her children than she thought possible in Northern Ireland. 'You still have to run with the Christian thing which I didn't want, but Mill Strand was absolutely fine, in terms of making the children feel part of it. As a governor, in terms of policy papers, when we talked of children of both traditions and others, I'd say could we just throw in the none there please. And I wasn't pooh-poohed. That was the first platform I had where I didn't feel completely odd.'

The rural parent, well away from both the north coast's mix of academic and student lifestyles around the university campus in Coleraine, and Belfast's comparative anonymity, said wryly of her very different surroundings, 'You're up against it from the start if you say you want to play the Christian thing down. You'd be pagans to a lot around here. Most of them probably want the school described as religious rather than not religious. And then NICIE have pinned their Christian colours to the mast.'

This was a teasing reference to the NICIE statement of principles issued in 1991, after consultation with all the existing integrated schools, as NICIE points out. Subsequent greenfield schools have been asked to sign up to the principles: it is a matter of considerable concern and even anger among some that no similar pledge was required of the schools that have since been declared 'transformed'. The anger comes from appreciation that the NICIE principles included specific obligations to nurture each child in his or her parents' religious and cultural traditions and to accord equality of status for the two main ethno-religious communities of Northern Ireland. Many of those who suspect transformation is an insufficiently monitored process with minimal requirements, think these NICIE stipulations set precisely the kind of standard that transforming schools should be asked to meet.

There are others in established integrated schools – teachers, governors and parents – who bridled at the primacy the NICIE principles gave to Christianity. Some of the same people, however, approved of the stipulations about maintaining a 40 per cent each Catholic and Protestant share of the first-year intake, as of teaching staff and governors. There is still widespread acceptance, it seems, that the rule first proposed by Tony Spencer is the only way to ensure a genuine balance and protect a minority from assimilation.

Appearances suggest that the most lively discussions on religious issues in integration are not now taking place around the question of Catholic children making First Communion with the other schools in the parish, if that ever indeed was central. Schools are still grappling with, or delaying grappling with, the representation of religious difference inside the school. In some, cheerful pragmatism seems to have dominated from the earliest days. A Lagan pupil of recent vintage can still repeat the school's Assembly version of the Lord's Prayer, a straight barter: Catholic 'who art' instead of Protestant 'which art', plus at the end the Protestant 'extra bit' as Catholics call it: 'for Thine is the Kingdom, the power and the glory'. It is Protestant sensitivity rather than that of Catholics which causes most hesitation. Shifts of emphasis and flashes of divergence are visible. For instance, when the Spires Primary in Magherafelt, County Londonderry, announced only three years after it started that it now had enough pupils for all years from first to seventh, principal Paul Trainor felt confident enough about local attitudes to invoke the once dangerous-sounding 'pluralism' rather than Christian-centredness. Parents, he said, clearly recognised the benefits of children being taught in a 'pluralistic and caring environment'. One of Lagan's earliest and perhaps best-organised regular school occasions – in a school others feel leans too heavily on ceremony – is the annual Lenten Ash Wednesday service, in which Catholic pupils and staff receive ashes on the forehead while the rest of the school looks on. Several other schools also mark Ash Wednesday, as a way of demystifying a Catholic ritual that for many Protestants was one of the most striking customs marking a whole community off as strangely, even threateningly, alien. But Lagan's blithe assembly of the entire school for the occasion is not the practice in Brownlow, for example, still feeling its way towards ceremony that suits an institution in the process of transformation.

'Those who wish attend,' says Brownlow's Brian O'Kelly. 'It's a reasonable number, and the teachers who attend include Catholics and Protestants.' Not all of his Catholic colleagues, he jokes, are very keen on the idea. The school has included questions about Ash Wednesday in surveys of pupil attitudes, asking 'Would you be interested in spectating in religious services other than your own (examples: Ash Wednesday, Harvest, Ramadan, Chinese New Year, et cetera)? Would you be interested in receiving information about special events in other religions (say at assemblies)?' Some in greenfield schools, not all of them 'purists', in the rather disparaging term sometimes used by officials and even by others inside the sector, are concerned that any school calling itself integrated is still asking what its practice should be on what they consider fundamental issues. The Brownlow question about interest in various religions finishes: 'Would you like to be told about what other pupils believe in?'

Yet although many of the original founders of integrated schools thought they were investing in a movement that would start out by telling pupils what others believed in, the better to promote mutual respect, it has never been easy to yoke principle to practice. As many products of Lagan confirm, the flagship did not convince all its pupils that it wanted to reflect a wide range of beliefs (Chapter 5).

Teachers there and elsewhere voice concern that as in other schools across the range, ambitions may have often outreached performance; others ask if it can ever be a bad thing to set goals high.

Integrated schools are the product of a bitty history and change from year to year, as does any good educational establishment. There is perhaps more dynamism, for good or ill, and certainly more diversity, than in either of the old established sectors; the most recent integrated school to start from scratch is Sperrin Integrated College, due to open in September 2002. Evaluating integrated schools, their practice, pupils, and the likely course of their future development, occupies a sizeable squad of researchers and academics, whose findings are pored over, disputed, and occasionally rejected by practitioners, sometimes welcomed, and pondered discreetly by government.

To some minds, the newer, small and still largely unexamined Irish-medium sector may have the edge in organisation and coherence. But then as a teacher in an integrated school with some experience of the Irish sector commented, 'There's a big difference between the two. You can measure the output of the Irish schools: do the children learn Irish? And they do, you can hear them. How do you measure the effectiveness of integrated schools? What is there that you can measure?' He still thought integration well worth his time and effort.

Each of the greenfield integrated schools emerged from a different group of founders, some involving teachers who went on to become the first principals. Origins explain a considerable amount of what distinguishes one school from another, the rest results from the process of defining integrated education, interpreted in different ways by different teachers on the ground in class, and by principals with widely varying approaches to the 'ethos' their school should have. Terminology engrosses some but leaves many cold: for most teachers, 'ethos' is not a word that trips off the tongue without a degree of embarrassment and self-mockery. NICIE's set of principles provide a short cut. But there are shades of disagreement about the Christian-centredness of the NICIE formula.

Others think the central word for the sector should be

'integrating' rather than 'integrated', a point made most forcefully by Brian O'Kelly, Brownlow's vice-principal for integration. For him as for others, integration is a continuing, demanding process; the word 'process' has become nearly as familiar among some of the most reflective teachers as it is in current Northern Ireland politics.

Several integrated schools work at including all staff in discussions, bringing caretakers, cleaners and canteen workers into training days as part of the school family. But this seems more an enthusiasm on the part of individual principals than an organic development. On the lips of many principals and other teachers, 'staff' more often means teaching staff than the entire workforce. Many are aware that in the busy school day and year, there is simply not time or opportunity enough to work on staff development: some are more insistent on the idea than others. It is only one of the areas where many think that a stronger and more authoritative central organisation could help (Chapter 6), indeed might be essential for the shape of future development.

STRUCTURE

Relationships between founders and teaching staff are often intense, and have been difficult more often than is healthy for the sector as a whole, say many. The presence of large numbers of parents on boards of governors disturbs a considerable number of teachers, though others accept, even welcome, the pattern as inseparable from the sector's history. Perhaps the greatest number, both those who worry about the potential for trouble between boards and school staffs and some less concerned by that issue, think that there is no 'sector as a whole', and they argue for a central body to give coherence, a sense of stability, and essential protection and guidance to teachers and principals.

'You do go through hell,' said one principal, insisting that she had enjoyed a good relationship with her board of governors through several changes of personnel, but was still bruised by experience. 'It bears no relation to the other sectors. You try for as jovial a relationship as you can, especially with your chairman, but it can all go terribly wrong.' Teachers face the next phase of development with emotions as varied as they are themselves. 'Things are going well for me at the minute,' said another principal, 'but you fear it won't always be good days – until governors are trained, and NICIE becomes an employing body, principals will live with fear to a great degree.'

A mixture of defensiveness about the limits of integrated education, a strain of idealism and a dash of uncertainty were detectable among teachers from an early stage. In 1989 the newly appointed principal of Braidside Integrated Primary, Ballymena, John Moulden, told a local newspaper, 'I don't think anyone is sure of where the movement is going. I only know that it seems to be an ultimately more hopeful way of educating children.' He wondered if the changes announced by the direct rule minister for education, Brian Mawhinney, welcomed by many, might not 'make the process too easy. The strength of integrated education is that parents take the initiative and want it to occur. The struggle is the valuable thing.'

The uncertainty identified by Moulden is still widespread, perhaps more acute at the moment than it has been for some years. In part this results from the government's promotion of transformation (see pages 48–56). 'A dilute form of integration,' says one longtime supporter sadly. The other innate weakness, some say, is a direct consequence of the haphazard way in which integrated schools emerged. The high proportion of parents on boards of governors of integrated schools is a legacy of their foundation, by groups that were largely made up of parents. Schools approved as viable by DENI can have ten or more parent members on the board of governors, including six formally designated as 'foundation governors,' so that it is possible for parents to make up a clear majority of the board. It is also possible for foundation governors to serve on boards for many years past the point where their own children leave school. This is fine when the governors are professional and disciplined, their interests primarily those of the entire enrolment and the school as a whole, say principals, teachers and others involved.

It is not so positive a factor, many judge, where there are personality clashes from the outset, or where parents confuse concern for their own child's progress with the necessity to be updated on school management by the principal inside board meetings. A total of nineteen principals have left their posts prematurely, according to their peers; 'forced out one way or the other', says one somewhat harassed survivor. Others insist stress was not a factor in all nineteen cases and point out that several principals have left to pursue careers elsewhere. The case made by integrated principals is supported by outside experts such as teachers' union representatives. The rate of wastage, they confirm, is disproportionate to the size of the sector.

There is widespread acceptance that 'the problem about the governors' comes directly from the origins of the 'integrated movement', except that few are convinced that 'the movement' amounts to a substantial and coherent organisation. 'The trouble with the principals and the boards usually arises out of confusion between the boundaries and the separate roles of management and governance,' says a friendly, but by now increasingly concerned observer. 'Trouble is that there is no agency that principals or board members can go to that's an impartial broker, and that has any authority.'

For some this is an argument that NICIE should be a statutory body like an education and library board or, more likely, CCMS. For others, the fact that NICIE is not acceptable now as an arbitrator argues against its transformation into a more important body. 'The first problem at the minute is that NICIE is seen as too close to many of the parents, the founding parents who've got schools up and running in many cases, with NICIE holding their hands. Even if it had statutory powers, the personnel and the links are a big part of the problem.' The speaker is widely regarded as one of the most successful principals, who has by and large had a smooth relationship with governors, with no personal disaster to distort her view.

Her remark about overlapping personnel is a useful reminder of how integrated education began and why it has been able to regenerate, as well as pointing to one cause of inevitable trouble. There remains a quality about many schools that began 'over a conversation in someone's kitchen', which is to many minds distinctive and cherishable. It is also clear, with hindsight, that the seeds of future trouble were also there in a dozen kitchens alongside the dynamism that launched the sector, perhaps even were an intrinsic element of that dynamism.

'Sheila appointed all the part-time teachers herself – I don't know whether I totally approved of that, but anyway,' says Maeve Mulholland, one of the two parents who first discussed setting up the school that became Lagan College. She remembers interviewing applicants for the first teaching posts: 'Sheila Greenfield was so impressive – that was a wonderful experience.' The tones are familiar from many other founder parents, clearly staggered to find themselves selecting, and employing, the people who would be teaching their children.

Before the teacher-interviewing stage there was wearying fund-raising that varied from baking buns and running raffles to formal, nerve-wracking approaches to charitable trusts and civil servants, as well as the scrubbing toilets and cleaning corridors that has become a hackneyed way of describing how much the original groups put into starting up schools. For many, scrubbing floors and walls of derelict buildings was followed by months of cleaning and care-taking before new, struggling schools were able to employ any nonteaching staff. 'She's a wonderful woman, the principal,' said another of the Millennium Primary School at Carryduff, south of Belfast, set up in the year 2000 with a total of ten children. 'But I think she's mad, there's no secretary, no caretaker, she does the cleaning herself. She's all right now but if it goes on like this ...'

The intensity of setting up schools is for many of those involved an unrepeatable experience: too strange and too exhausting for most to want to repeat it, but also a period they remember with nostalgia and great pride. 'It was far and away the biggest thing that ever happened in my life, apart from having my children, and maybe getting married,' one woman says, only slightly jokingly, about her membership of a group that set up a primary school. Her group, like others, spent months hacking away at the questions of how to teach religion and whether Christianity should be central or not; how historical and political controversy should be handled; whether and how Irish should be taught; and what attitudes should be to the display of flags and emblems in school. All of this ran parallel to an inconclusive debate about the school's policy on competition, prizes, and the eleven-plus.

Interviewing itself has meant a great deal to many in founder groups. In conservative, hierarchical Northern Ireland, teachers for a long time and for too many people were almost a superior caste, not to be questioned, or not to be questioned with impunity. The idea of choosing teachers, and of being party to employing them, has been a vital if sometimes unspoken element in parents' thinking of integrated schools as new and different – being set up by parents without reference to any hierarchical body, and shaped by them from the outset. 'For a lot of those people, the actual teachers they hired were always going to be Johnny-come-latelies,' said an educationalist brought in at one point to give expert advice. 'Two or three had a pretty clear picture of the kind of school they wanted, and there was never much chance of them finding teachers who could or would deliver it.'

Some of those involved realise that others have done similar things, against similar or even greater odds. The parents who set up the first Irish schools in Catholic west Belfast, for example, faced equal scepticism about their plans, won far less publicity from the wider world, and none of the backing from big names in showbiz, or from anyone with local political clout until the arrival of a Sinn Féin education minister. But the personal effort and commitment founder parents of integrated schools showed, and still show, lives in memories. It is not easily translated, for some, into a lower-intensity and less frenetic relationship with the day-to-day life of a school.

Many are more than happy to deliver their children to these new institutions and walk away, but some have always wanted much more. The slog for greenfield schools of getting started has always involved difficult discussion, especially in the early stages when few were sure what they meant by integrated education, and how it might be achieved – though many would say these questions are still open. Having argued passionately and long, frequently without an outcome that seemed clear or workable, it is hardly surprising that some parents later found it impossible to stand back when the 'hired hands' arrived. As many involved would readily admit, they did not and do not believe they should have to stand back.

Integrated education from the start was parent-driven: how could parents thereafter be expected to take a lesser role? Outsiders are often brisk about what they consider self-indulgent agonising from the integrated sector, about balancing the rights of principals, governors, parents, and pupils, and the tussles that ensue. A former principal in a controlled school who works now as an adviser to schools with problems says, 'Principals if they're honest will tell you the thing to say at the outset is "It's my school, I run it, OK have we got that? Now we'll get on fine if we all remember that."'

Some in the sector, perhaps more than the most outspoken champions of parents' rights recognise, are comparatively relaxed at that kind of line. As a temporary 'outreach' worker for NICIE, Ian McKay's job is to liaise with schools and with groups of parents hoping to start schools. He is also a parent governor in Braidside Primary, Ballymena, and is a bluff, good-humoured pragmatist. No one's idea of a pushover, he believes that when 'professionals' do their job well they deserve respect, and he is willing to allow that management needs a teaching professional's guidance more than that of lay governors. The very word 'professional' alienated some in the first wave of integrated parents, and is still an irritant. 'My own view is very simple,' McKay says. 'I'm a great believer in rendering unto Caesar. The principal is employed by the board of governors. I know nothing about teaching or running a school. He does. Therefore, you tell me what you think, principal, and if I agree with you I'll go along with you.'

Anne Murray, principal of Oakgrove Primary in what the two integrated schools there call L'Derry, says a dual element is unique to the sector: 'How we handle this is important, that we build mutual respect. We are parent-driven. Without parents we wouldn't exist: very strong parents, articulate. And the principals are often unusual too, people who stepped outside the tribe to some degree. There's potential trouble in that combination from the start.'

Others take a brisk, no-nonsense line: 'What's needed is for the principals themselves to be up to the job, and assertive about what that job is. You get very strong governors: in comes this poor innocent and they'll tear them apart unless it's clear to them what the difference between governing and management is. They've got to be forced back: no one gives up power willingly. And the only person who'll do that is the principal.' It was a display of utter confidence from the principal of an established and successful integrated school. But not long after another principal pointed to the confident one, with clear affection and concern, as an example of someone 'who's running into trouble at the minute by being too direct'.

In the early days, some teachers were convinced that their first customers included a remarkably high number with children who had educational problems of one kind or another: 'a bunch of seriously dysfunctional kids', says one ruefully of the first class he taught. The caricature of the integrated lobby at secondary level, as made up of dissatisfied middle-class parents of children rejected by grammar schools, always contained some truth. A significant number of parents who started integrated primary schools or who came to them early in their history had already been disappointed in other schools or were about to send children to school for the first time, fired with zeal to provide for them an entirely new Northern Ireland educational experience.

Inside the new set-up – for both sides of the adult equation whatever about the first pupils – an inevitable disappointment and degree of dismay loomed. Most staff in the new schools had been trained in Northern Ireland, many in the effectively segregated teacher training colleges, and until this point had taught in traditional schools, in which they themselves had been educated. 'Some of the first people in left again pretty quickly,' says one of the first to be recruited, who is still working in the sector and is an unswerving supporter. 'In 1985, they couldn't hack the integrated ethos. All this stuff about deep parental involvement and child-centredness on top of bringing Protestant and Catholic together. That was hard to take, if you were an ordinary teacher brought up on state school or maintained, like most of us were.'

The pioneers won some sympathy from colleagues in the established sectors, often in spite of considerable suspicion and even dislike of what the new sector stood for. 'The Sandal Mob, the Aran Sweater Brigade, that's what my friends called them,' says a now middle-aged veteran. She recalled friends in controlled schools 'robbing their storerooms to set me up in jigsaws, going up to their schools at night to get stuff', and an older Catholic friend 'cleaning out the cupboards of her infant room to set me up in Lego'.

Anthony Tomei of the Nuffield Foundation recalls occasionally chairing debates during the stormy period of developing schools immediately after the first phase. 'I thought once or twice this must have some of the flavour of the founding of the American state, when Virginia, Tennessee, et cetera sat down and said what can we all sign up to, what do we really believe in. Themes like the religious differences, there were various conferences held: I remember one, and there really were terrible, contingent problems.'

The basic rules had been drawn up by Tony Spencer originally as part of a draft prospectus for Lagan College in 1981: that all schools must be balanced in enrolment, in staffing and in their management, and that since integrated education must establish mutual respect between the embattled unionist and nationalist traditions, the balance must be set in terms of Protestant/Catholic representation. Tomei recalls:

One of the rules was no school should deviate from 60–40, on the face of it a sensible rule. But if you were starting a new school, with eighteen kids or twenty kids, and looking for a 60–40 ratio, and someone comes along – and you've got more Catholics than you have Protestants, so every Protestant is worth two Catholics – what do you do if you get a Buddhist? Do we turn a child away? These were real questions: really sharp here-and-now questions that tested these high-level principles. It was absolutely fascinating but incredibly difficult. What was incredible was that despite this huge amount of effort individual parents had put into individual schools, at some level there was another group of people who were prepared to compromise and to give up things which they obviously felt very strongly about, for a greater good. I suppose it was a combination of the individual vision of parents who wanted something different for their children here and now, which really drove it.

Tomei recognised the urgency in what at times might otherwise have seemed aimless and somewhat self-indulgent discussion. 'It wasn't anything abstract, it was *my* child tomorrow, next September. At the same time it was underpinned by this much larger vision, where people were prepared to make quite serious sacrifices: not compromises, sacrifices.'

It was never likely that teachers in schools whose underlying principles were forged in such intense debate could then proceed to teach as though anywhere else. These were, as one thoroughly sympathetic bystander observed, 'your original pushy parents'. Another who caught several glimpses of the arguments thought the debate on 'child-centred education sounded rather strange – it was all a bit old hat already in England, but people were very passionate about it in Belfast.' But as 'outsiders' eventually tended to recognise, the entire educational system in Northern Ireland was as conservative as the rest of the society. It was hardly surprising that people engaged in trying to change one aspect should want to shift attitudes on others at the same time. On some agendas, sexism and racism were part of the discussion from an early stage: the new schools must fight these also, some parents argued with great force. Elsewhere, they were unmentioned.

For many teachers in integrated schools, trouble with parents began early and has been fairly continuous ever since, born for the most part of the high expectations created by an innovative form of education. Some have dealt with it much better than others, some have had less to deal with. According to a wide range of teachers at various levels, including principals of large and small schools founded at different periods, a considerable number of 'integrated parents' have always been reluctant to defer to a teacher's skills and judgement. Use by teachers of the words 'professionalism' and 'professional' produced immediate suspicion and the beginnings of opposition from a number in founder groups. They are by no means the majority of parents, and some teachers, including a few principals, insist that they have had no trouble beyond what would be expected in any kind of school.

As tends to be the case in school life, clashes from the start revolved around the most mundane issues. An early Lagan supporter recalls first principal Sheila Greenfield 'having to deal with people who slogged their guts out to set up the school or worked very hard to support it just after that, in the first few years. And then it was a case of "OK, you two, your child is not going to do Maths at this level because she isn't up to it." Which is not easy to say to anyone, but harder when parents are founder parents.' Even more difficult, came the afterthought, when the parents are on the board of governors.

PRINCIPAL PROBLEMS

A few in the integrated world try to suggest that the problem has been exaggerated. To that, one senior figure in an organisational role responds, 'There's no doubt it's a problem. We're developing schools we know to have a flaw – the interface between governance and management. In the last seven to eight years we've lost around eleven principals and deputy principals.' Several of these had left their posts for career reasons, the official acknowledged, but many 'have been lost through what principals would say is boards which have too many and too strong parents'.

One principal says, 'On my board at the minute there is not a single person apart from the teacher reps and myself who isn't a parent – but my chair is great and there hasn't been a problem.' Nominees from DENI should soon change the balance, she hopes, 'in the meantime, it's fingers crossed. They want to know everything from the fabric of the building to the nature of requisitions. On the controlled school board of governors, when I was rep for a time, people were half-asleep. They really didn't want to know details. It's not like that in integrated schools.'

The problem is well known to staff in the other sectors, many integrated teachers admit, with varying degrees of embarrassment. A veteran teacher in one of the bigger integrated schools says the reactions of colleagues in mainstream schools is 'pretty hard to take. You don't want to be going to industrial tribunals, as has happened. You're showing everyone that people in these schools are killing each other and it's meant to be a movement of mutual respect!' A principal who has the respect of many in integration and is known as a 'good, calm manager' thinks a beefed-up NICIE is no answer. 'That might destroy useful relationships – they're not the right people. Good people, but … it's inescapable intermeshing, we should have experts we could bring in, new blood. What's needed is a bigger organisation, with mediating expertise.' Across a spectrum of age and experience, and the geographical and chronological spread of schools, there is an admission that the complexity and closeness of personal relationships are complicating factors, probably inevitable in a movement with this kind of history. In several of the worst clashes, the complaint from the principals' side became more bitter in the knowledge that governors with whom they were in dispute had close connections with NICIE. In other cases, by contrast, it was the principals who had the NICIE ties.

'I remember meeting two other principals, one of them for the first time, and we were talking about this, and I said "I wonder who'll be the first of us to go." It was an awful cynical thing to say, but after being involved that long I knew I was right too. And one of the three of us was gone by Christmas. The school only opened that September: the principal lasted until Christmas and was driven out.' The school he named went on to change principals again, a pattern familiar elsewhere. When principals are gathered together, it produces a share of gallows humour. 'There's a theory out there that they get bloodthirsty, these governors. You know, "Next! Off with his head!" Unless they're absolutely perfect.' There was the slightest trace of hysteria in the joke. This was someone who felt particularly strongly about the most recent of his colleagues to fall foul of a board of governors: a friend, and former colleague.

Some brought trouble down on their own heads, it was admitted. But at their most pessimistic, teachers at different levels, not principals alone, say a parent majority on a board has to mean trouble. 'I think there's a huge amount of work to be done training governors,' says a still-energetic and -optimistic head. 'One major problem we have at the moment is that NICIE are doing their best, but the trainers are often quite young, with no integrated school experience. And the problems are distinctly different in our schools.'

The difference between parent governors in integrated schools and those on mainstream boards of governors, it is said, is not only that they are present in greater numbers but also that these are a particularly strong and assertive kind of parent. 'Too often, when they're governors, they forget that they're not there to talk about their own children,' says a principal who insists in general that parents must have a special place in integration. 'When it comes to "My child was told that Santa's not real, what's your policy on Santa Claus?" Or "My daughter isn't allowed to play football", and the board spends the next half an hour on it ... where does an individual interest legitimately become a policy discussion?'

A pioneer parent and governor in Lagan College recalls: 'It started early. There was the time someone invited deprived kids at the school to somewhere ritzy – in England, some posh school? Parents and teachers were to go with them. Sheila Greenfield asked who would be responsible for discipline. Both parents and teachers, the parents suggested. No, Sheila said, it had to be one or the other, it couldn't be a mix, and the thing didn't happen. People were very cross that she blocked it, though.'

In several cases, according to people involved, the differences that eventually resulted in a principal's departure began while schools were still at the planning stage. In one small town, there is a very public legacy of close friendships still bitterly sundered several years after such a row, of people walking past each other on the main street or refusing to speak in local shops. 'It was personalities dressed up in issues,' says one wounded ex-participant, who admits to having been 'not entirely blameless. First comes "I don't like the cut of their jib." Then it's "What do they believe? I don't like that, I'm not having that in our school."'

On several occasions, a central and divisive issue has been the eleven-plus examination. Principals hired in the belief that the integrated sector opposes selection and would not wish to see children entered or prepared for the examination, have discovered that parents are either split, or belatedly swinging to support it. A dedicated and talented supporter of integration who has been both a governor in several schools and a parent of integrated pupils, and who has advised both organisers and teachers as a specialist, looks back on difficult years at close quarters with the problems of several schools. As for others, involvement with integrated education has meant meeting and in many cases befriending a considerable number of people with idealism, talent and commitment: 'lovely people, great people. But sometimes I think that we've created a monster. In terms of the hurt, the damage – not just in one school or a few schools: there's a lot of fallout. I do sometimes sit and think about all the teachers, all the parents, who've fallen by the wayside disillusioned. Or broken, in some cases. There's so much pain that's been caused: that can't be right.'

There is one widely shared consolation: few, if any, of the most harrowing disputes have ever had anything to do with religious or political differences. 'It doesn't sound too good for supporters of integrated education to be tearing lumps out of each other,' one put a common belief pithily. 'But at least the divides aren't the obvious ones.'

A number of the less engaged participants, drawn in because they were hired in some guise or were asked for advice as experts, make the point that amateurism famously engenders heat. Voluntary groups are famous for their rows, they say, while the most purist political groups are a byword for furious, bitter splits. 'Maybe a lot of it comes back to not knowing how to run meetings,' a teacher sighs, exhausted by the process of getting a school off the ground, and then setting up classes in it. 'When you have a dozen parents in a room and a couple of well-wishers with a bit of expertise, someone with strong feelings is the chair and you run into the third hour –

then you're in trouble. No one makes sense when it goes on that long.'

From the start, the integrated world of endless discussion has witnessed tempers fray because of long-windedness, which, according to cooler minds, is the besetting sin of volunteers. The months of talk required to set up a County Down school are still vivid in the memory of a lifelong supporter of the principles of integrated education. He recalls with affection 'what a very good mix it was in class terms as well as religion. The other chief memory is exhaustion.' A professional educationalist who advised on schools in Tyrone and Fermanagh remembers: 'We operated on a consensus model: consensus by exhaustion. You were there until 1 or 2 in the morning until you reached it.'

Friction between the first professionals to join discussions and those who had already been debating with intensity for some time, might have been inevitable in any case. When those hired to come on board flexed muscle, there were clashes. 'On the continuum from "No parents beyond this point", we brought parents into the centre,' observes a now ageing activist. 'Perhaps this was the price to be paid. If principals could just be prepared for it.'

Solutions proposed include training for governors and principals, a more thoughtful and stringent approach to recruitment of principals, and, from several directions, the recommendation that a fixed term of headship might be worth considering. Many principals insist – and some at least of their counterparts in mainstream schools agree with them – that running an integrated school is distinctly different from running other schools, and therefore requires other qualities. 'You might need different principals for different stages of development,' said Olwin Frost, head of Oakwood Primary, at Derriaghy on the outskirts of Belfast. She makes a plausible case. 'It's a bit much to ask of just one person. You want someone who can represent the school. But remember it'll start small and grow, so you need a person who can be principal of a small school and principal of a large one, and have the experience to do both and do it well. You want a people person, who's really good with parents, and you need to be a sales person with the staff, with the world outside. The media profile is something a lot of people find very taxing, and it's an integral part of the job.' She laughs at the memory of one London trip. 'I never thought I'd be walking down Downing Street or on the stage at the South Bank speaking to thousands!'

INSIDE SCHOOLS

For all that organisational shortcomings, lack of support and comparative isolation perturb some schools, it is daily classroom life that preoccupies most teachers: the essential slog of teaching, with the added dimension of integration. Working at it, many say, is the rule, and they mean working on themselves and on colleagues as well as with children. From the most baffled, new and at a loss to the skilled, experienced and comparatively sophisticated, teachers in integrated schools tend to confess at some stage that they crave more time to 'work things out'. The cry is identical to that in all kinds of school, where pressure of work rules out thinking time, much less the 'staff development' that education authorities now routinely and ceaselessly demand.

In integrated schools, the penalties for not having time to develop are immediately obvious in classes. When they were offered a day's debriefing, teachers from a County Antrim school reported a battery of 'dilemmas' to trained community relations workers: 'Overheard someone calling another pupil an "Orange bastard"; in the playground children role-playing riots, police and protesters, based on Holy Cross; a pupil says his mum doesn't think he should talk to the police when they visit the school; a pupil asks the question, why do they not let the Orangemen march in Dunloy?'

The question about Dunloy must have seemed particularly sharp and difficult: another small County Antrim town, mainly Catholic, whose objections to a march led to a retaliatory, abusive and long-lasting picket of Mass-goers in a mainly Protestant town fifteen miles away. 'Responses' to the dilemmas sounded slightly desperate: 'Maybe take time later to explain; confront a situation you know more about; be confident from your own identity; come to colleagues for advice.' As for the 'Orange bastard' query, 'Label the behaviour, not the person,' was the most solid piece of advice: 'Don't say you're bad, say that's bad.'

The crying need many were expressing was clearly for time in school with more experienced colleagues, to ask for help and to work out attitudes. Some try to tackle the problem directly, without bringing in outside agencies. Ulidia is a second-level school which was finally recognised by Martin McGuinness as viable after subsisting on donations for three years. On the outskirts of strongly loyalist Carrickfergus, County Antrim, the school draws Catholic pupils from a considerable distance. Olwyn Griffith has special responsibility for development among a young staff. An experienced and passionate maths teacher, she followed two others to Carrickfergus from Lagan College, and is slightly nostalgic for a staff room where people knew each other well enough to joke about touchy subjects. 'Time has to be made for planned integrated activities, for want of a better word. We're planning a residential weekend, and people have pushed for it soon.'

For her, there is a unique and positive role parent governors should play in schools. Ulidia's newness is an antidote to reports of bruising experience elsewhere. Countering much of the darkness of other discussions, and showing none of the defensiveness, much less resentment of some teachers, Olwyn Griffith says founder parents 'have the vision', so it is they who must 'guard against it beginning to fade. They have to hold it close and very dear.'

The value of integrated education is something even the most concerned and exhausted teachers never question. One class in Ulidia provided this upbeat teacher with an example she will happily retell for years. They were discussing – in 'Ulidia Studies', the school's regularly timetabled period for debate – the argument at the Stormont Assembly between unionists and republicans about the republican wish to display Easter lilies in the Parliament building's stately entrance hall. Unionists objected, because the flowers commemorate the 1916 Rising against British rule, and republicans pointed out that Stormont itself was for decades a symbol of unionist domination. Olwyn Griffith's class knocked the subject back and forward, 'then a child who normally doesn't say very much asked "Didn't you say that lilies are a symbol of hope? I think they should be there, to hope that the Good Friday Agreement will work, so we can have peace and forget about the past."'

5
Pupils

They are the raw material, they become the visible product. Pupils in integrated schools are held up as case studies, examined as living testimonials to integrated education. The schools are subjected to flash floods of the world's press and what sometimes seems like a great boiling river of academics, some of whom conduct surveys over months or even take up residence for considerable periods. Hazelwood College in ever-simmering north Belfast has hosted one researcher for an entire year.

All the questions point in the same direction: Are pupils more tolerant because of their schooling? Do they have friends from outside their own community? Does integrated education work? A surprising number of current pupils deal patiently with many questioners, others deliver standard replies in school, and switch off when they get home. 'You got used to the TV cameras,' says one shy twenty-year-old. 'It was visitors I didn't much like. You'd show them round: Americans and Norwegians, people from all over the world. Some were lovely. English people were the worst, always asking had you made any friends from another religion, like you lived in a reservation or something. The worst I remember was this teacher, walking him up to see our music department, and he said he couldn't understand why we hadn't solved our religious problems: "We solved ours hundreds of years ago." I thought oh yes, like you solved your race problem and your class problem, and where do you think we got our problems from? But I couldn't very well say to him.'

Pupils report various reactions to the experience of VIP visits: being praised or interrogated by outsiders, used as photogenic, camera-friendly backdrops, or as cheap, supposedly insightful broadcast fodder for transient foreign journalists. Pressed to analyse the nature of their friendships and classroom exchanges, and the texture of their days, more than one otherwise tolerant adolescent responds occasionally with a put-down along fairly standard lines, with only slight modifications: 'It's just school, and you don't think about it, you just go.' Or, 'My friends are just my friends.' Some might think that taking friendship for granted across the divide of religion and communal background is in itself adequate witness to the simple power of integrated schooling, the sharing of childhood.

The promoters of integrated education have always been keen to offer pupils as advertisement, though twenty years into the story research has begun to suggest that no certainty is likely about the effects. It may not be possible to pin down the distinctiveness or essence of integrated education, some academics say, or to define what it does for children. The verdict, or nonverdict, will not surprise anyone who has ever listened to or tried to question very young people, particularly about schools. Going to school is an intense experience for some, boring for others, influenced by as many factors as there are people. Any honest and observant parent is aware that the experience of two siblings of the same school can differ, that one child's opinion of a class and teacher is often entirely dissimilar from that of another.

But the influence of the schools on extra-school and post-school life preoccupies some in the integrated sector itself, aware as they are of the hostility towards integrated education. When articulate pupils present the case for integration, there is a sigh of adult satisfaction that it sounds and looks better than a professional presentation, has the extra quality of artlessness, and cannot be queried like that of an adult. 'Strong men in tears,' said one tireless promoter of the sector, only slightly humorously of a trip by pupils invited as guest speakers to a New York dinner given by the Ireland Funds, another charity which has supported integrated education for years, where several spoke to an Irish-American audience. Yet arguably, a broadcast that provided critics with what they thought splendid ammunition has been among the most effective advertisements of all.

In 2001, on BBC Radio Ulster's most popular programme, the phone-in cum current affairs magazine *Talkback*, a fifth-former said, 'It's different when you're outside school, because then you're in your own area. It's really sectarian and nobody wants to hear you, so you just go along with everybody else.' She was describing the contrast between daily life in her integrated school, and throwing petrol bombs and stones, rioting at night; the rioters' targets were the neighbouring community, people in the next street. A boy said he did not riot, and he never would: 'I don't think it's right. You go to an integrated school and then you riot with people that you're friends with in school?' This was not the contribution that won notice, however.

What caught immediate and widespread attention, in subsequent angry, derisive and concerned phone calls and in the letters pages of local papers, was the girl's description of going out rioting. Did parents not notice the smell of petrol and smoke when the young people came home, the reporter asked. 'My family's out rioting with me,' the girl said, 'my mammy and daddy, friends and everybody, so everybody's out doing it.' Her mother would throw a petrol bomb or a stone? 'No, *she* wouldn't do that,' the girl answered, audibly smiling slightly. 'She would stand about.' Her mother watched: it was her father who threw things. 'It's just an everyday thing. That's the way I'm brought up and I'm not going to change and neither is anybody else.' From her tone of voice, it was hard to know whether she was more depressed or defiant about not changing.

Her innocent, open awareness that life in school and life at home took off at right angles to each other hit a public nerve. Clearly, the group in general saw contradictions between rioting and the atmosphere and spirit of their school, but not how to cut the ties of community, and of family. The whole exchange underlined the fact that integrated education is grafted on to other socialising agencies – family and street – but it does not replace them.

The discussion involved nine pupils of Hazelwood Integrated College: working every day, as shocked listeners immediately pointed out, in mixed classes of Protestants, Catholics and others, supposedly confronting prejudice and trying to build mutual respect. The broadcast caused the school some difficulty, and gave a considerable number of people unholy delight, including an official of the Catholic schools' administrative umbrella CCMS, who thought it questioned the worth of twenty years of integrated education. There was finger-pointing, however, even among those with no axe to grind. 'Bit embarrassing, eh?' an affluent Catholic teased a colleague involved in integrated education. Her own teenagers attend Methody, the big south Belfast grammar, because their parents consider it more prestigious than the Catholic grammars. 'They're so high and mighty in the integrated world,' she said, 'you can't help grinning when they come a cropper.'

Hazelwood principal Noreen Campbell went on air later to defend the pupils, and the school. Her argument in the main was that the openness of the teenagers proved the value of the school's work. The most remarkable feature of the broadcast was that local sectarian tensions and the fraught issues of policing and police bias were discussed calmly, outlined for the reporter, Marie-Louise Connolly, without anyone shouting anyone else down or being stung into a hostile reaction: more than most local politicians can manage.

The group was asked what the effects in school were when people came in with the smell of petrol still on their hands after rioting during the night. 'You just have to get along with everybody,' one girl said, 'and in school it's different. You go to an integrated school. Although you may be a bigot, you have to pretend to get along with everybody.' The reporter said, 'You're a Catholic and you're sitting beside a Protestant girl here. You'll have your lunch and your break with her, you'll have the normal girly chitchat with her during the morning. Can you go out tonight and throw petrol bombs at her or in the direction of her house? What do you feel about people that you know of that might attack her home?' The girl said matter-of-factly, 'I wouldn't do anything to her because she's my friend, I know her, I know everything about her. The people that we do riot with have just intimidated us out of our area.'

Another thought children looked as much to their peers as to parents. 'Communities should be sorted out before they integrate with other communities.' Why did she decide then to come to an integrated school, the reporter asked. 'I wanted to mix with the other side, and I feel it's right to do it during the day. But it is very hard to come into the school and integrate with the so-called other side when that night you're going out and you're fighting with them. I know on some levels that it's wrong, but rioting is a thing you do on the spur of the moment, when the tensions are high.'

Integrated education might work in the classroom during the day, pressed the reporter, 'but is it really working when you leave these classrooms, and you leave what you've been told in school, take your uniform off and go out rioting?' A girl said, very calmly, 'Integrated education *does* work. Everyone's sitting here getting along.' She admitted that the 'mentality that goes along with rioting, it obviously affects people. They'll come into school and they'll say "Were you at the riot last night?" They'll fight over it. But a lot of issues should be raised with the politicians who know what's going on in their own areas but they're not doing anything about it.'

But local adults have no idea what to do about sectarian tensions in north Belfast, beyond refuelling them or holding up their hands in horror. As this century begins, the Hazelwood schools sit perched on perhaps the most precarious of fault lines in the whole of Northern Ireland, where the most intractable phase of the political problem is likely to be played out in the immediate to middle future. A form of education devised to provide a shared childhood may find itself constantly at the centre of the political stage, having to operate where segregation is sharpest and regularly reinforced. These are precisely the conditions which critics of integrated education from the start foretold it could not withstand, indeed would not even try to confront. 'It's for kids who don't need it,' the critics said and still say. 'The middle class in mixed areas aren't fighting each other. How it's going to reach kids on the Falls and the Shankill?'

The two Hazelwoods, primary and secondary, are near each other in a part of north Belfast where population movements have been constant and full of contention, with Protestant and Catholic streets either side of the most irregular and untidy of peacelines. As changing demographic patterns further reduce the Protestant majority in the coming years, tensions are likely to increase rather than fade. Other schools in similar places, of course, have also been affected by the recent friction, as many have been for years past, some for much longer and more dramatically than the two Hazelwoods. At the height of the Troubles, it was routine for neighbouring state and maintained schools to stagger their closing and opening times to minimise stoning between their pupils. The most direct and most traumatic experience in recent years has been that at Holy Cross Primary, standing among Protestant housing beside Catholic Ardoyne, where Catholic parents and children were abusively picketed as they went to and returned from school. When Holy Cross flared up again at the start of 2002, other local schools were also threatened, most of them Catholic.

As the trouble began, a Catholic mother said on camera that she was shocked to see children from the local integrated school she worked in, clearly Hazelwood, among the loyalist picketers. The remark instantly switched some attention from Holy Cross to Hazelwood. Two subsequent incidents drew more: the loyalist killing of twenty-year-old Catholic postman Danny McColgan, who had been a pupil at both the Hazelwood Primary and the secondary, and the fatal traffic accident near the primary school when a fifteen-year-old Protestant, Thomas McDonald, was knocked down and killed as he cycled out of the Catholic Longlands Road. In both schools, people shy away from public comment on the two tragedies and their effects. The district is simply too volatile: the least said the better.

Throughout months of sporadic but often intense trouble on the streets, the Hazelwood bus continued to pick up pupils from both the Shankill and Ardoyne. But both schools think they have begun to notice an effect on applications for 2002–2003 places. 'Some people are going back into their own community,' a teacher said. 'There are kids going from our primary to the nearest Catholic secondary, and I'm sure in another year they'd have been sent to us.' In an area that regards itself as under attack from 'the other side', mixing is even less popular than usual when feelings are particularly high. It is of course during exactly this kind of period that some become desperate at the prospect of their children becoming locked into conflict, and decide even more definitely that they want them to mix, and not to spend all their time with friends of their own religion.

For all that the original site for Lagan was next door to a comparatively modest Protestant housing estate; its proximity to affluent south Belfast fitted hostile preconceptions and was a gift to the naysayers. There was a kernel of accuracy in the attacks. Leaving aside the fatuous, smug notion that there is no middle-class prejudice to confront, the integrated education lobby has always known that if parental demand across Northern Ireland is to be met, schools have to be reachable from the most segregated districts, though they would be useless if built inside them. No one much fancies bussing as a solution, but in many places pupils still travel considerable distances to the nearest integrated school. Some schools are in mainly middle-class districts; some, like the two Hazelwoods on Whitewell Road, are very definitely not.

Pupils at the primary and secondary alike come from a distance, picked up by buses, delivered by parents in cars, with many from nearby streets, a mix in themselves of social classes and of Protestant and Catholic, sometimes bitterly opposed. When people on both sides of the integration debate talk about the need to change sectarianism and bridge the divide, or the implausibility of integrated schools having any effect, it is places like this that spring to mind as the most difficult and challenging, their conflict the product of more than a century's fear and dislike between two groups. The BBC reporter talked to the Hazelwood group because trouble had been more or less constant for months. Riots regularly broke out in the early evening in Ardoyne, in the small loyalist Glenbryn beside it (which looks to the bigger, older Shankill as its parent district), on the Limestone Road about a mile away, and along the irregular, messy, multiple interfaces further out of the city, around Whitewell.

Ardoyne is where the Troubles first erupted in 1969, in streets which had also seen trouble in the 1920s. The Limestone Road has similarly been a front line between poor Protestants and Catholics for decades, and the Whitewell Road is a line through almost suburban estates, inhabited by many families decanted from old streets closer into the city. During 2001, a large number of loyalist pipe bombs were thrown into Catholic homes around the Limestone Road, clearly organised, after a fashion, by the para-military UDA. Splinter republican groups were occasionally suspected of gunfire among rioting Catholics, but police and other paramilitaries agreed that as in Ardoyne, the IRA had clearly clamped down on rioters, was neither leading nor encouraging violence, and had decided not to retaliate against the UDA. The motive force of much of the violence was loyalist, essentially unpolitical and bereft of strategic thinking.

Trouble in the new century follows the patterns of the past, with a latter-day twist. North Belfast was once Protestant-dominated, its Catholic minority less able to find work or tending to be employed in less secure and worse paid jobs, while strongly Protestant trade unions controlled access to apprenticeships in the shipyard and better-paid light engineering generally. The municipal worthies of the north side of the city – the owners of most major businesses, the bulk of representatives on the city corporation, later Belfast City Council – were Protestant and unionist. Many Protestants lived in comparative poverty, but the comparison that mattered was with even poorer Catholics. Over the past twenty years, affluent Protestants have fled north Belfast, leaving the old and disadvantaged behind. Economically and politically, power locally is increasingly nationalist and Catholic.

For people who possessed very little more than their fellow Christian neighbours of a different denomination, for whom life was also hard, and who lived in similar cramped and insanitary housing, belief in Protestant superiority and Catholic inferiority helped in the past to justify inequalities and unfairness. For Protestants who have grown up in a Northern Ireland which in recent years has changed at a bewildering speed, and in which Catholics are ever more clearly the ascendant community, it can be difficult if not impossible to know who to believe about the past. Unquestioned assumptions have drifted away in a fog of denial, drowned out by the hubbub of the Troubles or blurred by change. In north Belfast, as elsewhere in Northern Ireland, the new face of power reflects an underlying demographic shift. The sharpening of segregation patterns, the gradual shrinkage of a once-marked Protestant majority, and a general Protestant migration eastwards and out of north, south and west Belfast, all pose serious political questions for the future, and will make it increasingly difficult for integrated schools in a number of areas to achieve or retain a balanced enrolment. North Belfast may be the most stark and dramatic arena, but others witness a milder version of the new power play.

A teacher who became involved years later in the effort to transform Brownlow High School in Craigavon into the integrated Brownlow College, hotly opposed by unionists, grew up in working-class Protestant north Belfast. He is married to a Catholic, and his interest in integrated education is a mix of loathing for the eleven-plus and the selective system, and a wish to see an end to segregation generally. His parents were often short of money and his mother was a regular visitor to the pawnshop. He knew they were little better off than Catholic neighbours but remembers the moment when he recognised a difference. 'We were on a bus in

Corporation Street and we passed the dole queue. My da said they were men out of work. Then he said "And most of them are Catholics." I asked why and he said, "that's just the way it is."' For this teacher, as for many others, his adulthood into middle age has been dominated by the Troubles and sectarian division. His own children were settled in mainstream schools before Brownlow emerged, but having spent his own professional life in similar schools, he has enough civic spirit to wish a new form of education for the children of others.

The attempt to transform Brownlow was sparked by demographic trends – the development of a local Catholic majority. Brownlow might resemble Hazelwood more than any of the other integrated schools in its social mix, though several rural schools come close. In many schools, the desire to deny the accusation of being for the 'posh', and being unduly middle-class, has battled with a desire to show that they can achieve academic success and maintain discipline. In the struggle, the original promise that integrated education would unite children of all abilities, as well as across divides of religion and culture, has been strained, sometimes beyond breaking point.

The schools take varying attitudes to mixed-ability teaching. In Lagan, policy over the years gradually produced a regime that some teachers say can still deliver integration as envisioned but that others think has lost its original distinctiveness, and promise. A recent ex-pupil says, 'I think Lagan has no claim to a hallowed position. It sold out to get good grades: to an extent they abandoned their ideals.' The description of streaming and its effects comes in very similar form from a variety of ex-Laganites. It is countered by some teachers past and present, who stress the difficulties in teaching mixed-ability classes, and by several ex-pupils who left early because they found lessons made messy 'by people who didn't want to learn', as one put it, or by 'teachers who weren't able to handle the classes'.

Several described what to them seemed like two separate schools inside one, divided not by religion but by streaming for academic ability. 'Yes, you mixed all right. But once you were streamed in one of the lower groups, you got the crap teachers, and if you get the crap teachers you're going to rebel: smoke and skip class. So then you don't get the same educational opportunity, you don't get the results, and you go back to the same background as before. It's all one religion and one politics, and you have no chance of a decent job.' This was a twenty-three-year-old who thought his own comparative academic success was largely due to middle-class expectations at home, though he admitted there were 'some brilliant teachers in Lagan'. His dominant emotion, however, was anger on behalf of less wealthy friends, lost to him in the first few years of school when 'streaming kicked in. After that the only ones who made it were the most determined, only one or two of them. Beyond that, the people who sounded like me and the people from the Ormeau Road, Twinbrook, from the Protestant estates near the school, we hardly mixed at all. On the bus, maybe, and I felt embarrassed then by my accent.'

For some pupils, Lagan was a disappointment because to them it lacked the radical edge they thought an experimental and pioneering effort ought to have: indeed it seemed staid and conservative. 'I suppose I resented that it wasn't a neutral place, a welcoming place for the non-Christians, or humanists,' says Hugh Odling-Smee, son of Anne, longtime champion of integration, whose first year there was the school's fifth. 'I think sometimes that Lagan College took a wrong turn: it became much more rigid, more like a grammar school.'

But unlike the angry young man who saw two different schools in one, Hugh was convinced that Lagan brought classes together. 'The most positive thing I can tell you about Lagan College, the best thing about it was class – it was across the board classwise. I grew up in Malone and all my friends came from Malone, because I went to primary school there. The fact that I was meeting people from west Belfast, Twinbrook, and also Ballybeen estate, Tullycarnet – that was the best thing, the number one best thing, because it told me that people were people essentially wherever you go. That sounds very facile but it was important to me, that you could go to west Belfast and people were just like you, and you had something in common with them: that divisions along geography and class lines weren't important. To me it wasn't religion: I didn't care if someone was Catholic or Protestant. But before I went I did sort of care about what sort of class people were. And my illusions were utterly shattered: so I found that middle-class people can be utterly idiotic, and working-class, or what New Labour call low-paid people were, well, people were people. Where else in Belfast would I have got that? Hazelwood, maybe.'

To former and indeed present pupils in other integrated schools, Hazelwood's open discussion of raw division on the streets is desirable perhaps, but not their experience. 'We don't talk much about touchy stuff,' said a fifteen-year-old at a school west of the Bann. 'It's not open enough in classes. Only one or two teachers will get a debate going, but a lot of us don't say much.' It was a reminder of teachers who confess that conversation in the classroom is far from easy on political and religious subjects. 'You need training in this stuff and back-up,' as one said. 'You can't just jump in with a class, especially if you don't know who'll back you up if it all goes wrong.'

The fall-back position for many, if pupils are to be believed, is to teach their subjects as best they can with minimal cross-reference to Northern Ireland's division, plus emphasis throughout the school on the unifying aspects of religion. A running complaint about Lagan from present and former pupils echoes that from some other, later schools: that they are too Christian-centred, to the exclusion or at least the belittlement of other faiths and, especially, of atheists and agnostics. 'The ecumenical Christianity in Lagan really was cloying, unreal. There were a lot of services that weren't appropriate,' says one ex-pupil. 'We were always praying for something,' comments another. 'The amount of time you spent in the chaplaincy was ludicrous, sitting around. Though the chaplains were nice women, and the occasional man – they were maybe the most liberal people in the staff, looking back.'

Put it to the disgruntled that this was the stuff of integration, surely, supervised or gently guided discussion in an unthreatening environment, and some react badly. 'But we didn't do the differences between Protestants and Catholics, the touchy stuff, sectarianism. In Lagan they didn't mention politics. If anyone mentioned a shooting or something like that teachers would shush them. You got arguments in the classroom when the teacher was out, people saying Was there was fighting in your street last night, Yeah, we were rioting, Huh, we'll handle you', but it didn't go anywhere. When there was a bomb, we had silence. In assembly. We were always having silences. You were supposed to pray in your head.'

The school's practice of taking the younger pupils to visit a variety of churches went down badly, but then these were not religious students: 'they all began to blur'. Several were gripped, however, by one minister in particular, serving a largely tough loyalist estate not far from Lagan, who came to the school as a part-time chaplain. He made more impression, even on those least interested in religion, than teachers who shied away from possible controversy.

Others have different memories. 'Mr Donaldson was great: you talked about everything you wanted to. He made a class on religion into everything. Sometimes you'd hear people starting to get mad but he would just kind of gentle it along.' Clearly, as in most schools, teachers made the difference. Even the most uncomfortable with what they saw as Lagan's 'cloying' Christianity were lyrical about a number of teachers. One of the ex-pupils who was most dismissive about the school's failure, in her eyes, to open up discussions, talked fondly about four or five teachers as inspirational. She also treasured the one friendship she had maintained across an originally wide class and cultural divide, describing how with another girl she 'would corner Sharon [not her real name] about marching on the Twelfth: we'd get her to talk about why other people didn't think walking up and down beating drums was so great.' A valuable experience, then? 'That was outside class, nothing to do with the school.' It was a harsh, young judgement, since the school provided the environment and, as teachers will often admit, the hardest things cannot be taught: they are learned, if the environment is right.

A measure of disappointment with Lagan may have more to do with unrealistic expectations about integration, adult observers of the school suggest, than with failings in teaching or the construction of an ethos. Some of the most critical are children of veteran supporters, who have also been to integrated primary schools. As one otherwise fond parent noted drily, 'They have no idea what other schools are like, what it would be like to be the tiny minority of Catholics in a big Protestant school, say. And since they were tiny they've been listening to the adults they know best talking about integration, joining in. Put that together with the normal discontent of being a teenager, and it's hard to imagine what would satisfy them.'

A band of ex-Lagan opinion is echoed however, among pupils from several of the other integrated schools in their concern that there is no respect or even recognition of those who are 'not mainstream Christians, not Muslim or Hindu or Buddhist, but atheists from here', as one said. 'Isn't it sort of specially important now after the Good Friday Agreement, isn't this what we should be part of building – a neutral space where people can be not Catholics, not Protestants? There are a lot of people who want that.'

In Drumragh College, Omagh, in 2001 a group of fifth years wrote about their reactions to the school, a method some teachers favour before tackling discussion in class. What pleased this group had made little or no impression on the discontented Laganites, or was outside their experience. These were teenagers whose previous school life had been entirely segregated. One wrote:

> Before attending Drumragh, I was a pupil at Loreto Convent Primary, an extremely Catholic school. Throughout primary school, I never once considered there was another religion. For me Catholicism was the only way to live. I am not saying integration has changed my faith but I do feel I was sheltered from ever discussing other Christian beliefs.
> I think that honestly before I was oblivious and ignorant of the Protestant community. My cousins in Belfast always filled me with a view that we are different: 'stay with your own'. It is obvious to me that some people would rather not make the effort to mix and

share their backgrounds with the 'other side' and for these people I pray.

A less rosy but ultimately positive view came from another girl in the class. 'I have seen two friends fight over their religion. The two boys haven't spoken since second year now and will never have the chance because one has left the school. But this was the only time I saw or heard of any religious fighting.' For her, one of Drumragh's most striking virtues was its cherishing of pupils with disabilities 'who I probably would not have met except through school'. But she also thought she had gained skills that would help 'in the workplace or university – I have learnt not only what religions have in common, I've also learnt to respect everyone's opinion and how to avoid unnecessary arguments. In some ways I have been given an extra education.'

The theme of understanding integration as inclusive of all abilities as well as cultures and religious beliefs came through again in a third Drumragh view, this time from a boy who found that 'groups where some people have learning disabilities made me take my time and help others. I've also been working with people who are very smart, good at sports, and very good actors, and I have learned to like people for what they are good at … people always have something good about them.'

Nóra Murray-Cavanagh is in her second year at university in Edinburgh, certain that her integrated school gave her a way of seeing and dealing with Northern Ireland that she would not have gained from education in either of the other sectors. When asked in Scotland to explain the politics of Northern Ireland she finds herself endlessly qualifying assertions about party stances or the origins of particular disputes. 'I say, but that's not what other people think.' She believes she owes awareness of difference to her own background and her parents Anne and Colm, who helped start the integrated education movement in Derry which produced the two Oakgrove schools. Nóra elaborates on her position:

> There was this guy from Newcastle I met the other day. When he heard where I was from we got talking about the Bloody Sunday

films. He asked what I thought, and I told him there was a huge problem there, whatever I wanted to believe I was biased anyway. A lot would present it as a communities' conflict, whereas in an integrated school I think that we believe that it's a community that has problems within itself. We don't want a division.

Where I live in Derry, with a huge Catholic population, I would have gone to a Catholic school. Yet from the sheer experience of not meeting Protestant, unionist, whatever, people with those opinions, it would be alien for me, it would be scary, something I don't think I would have very much respect for. But luckily I had lots of people working on my behalf to make sure that I got a broader view of things.

It's not necessarily specific things. It's what you don't experience by not having the opportunity if you're in a segregated community, housing estate, school, whatever. It's just that you grow up to believe that there's a difference, and maybe just by seeing that there's no difference, or that the differences aren't too big to overcome, you can celebrate diversity and all that. A good friend of mine that I went to school with, his uncle was killed on Bloody Sunday. In the same class, friends with me and this other person, you have someone whose father worked as a police forensic scientist.

Once we were having a party and we're fifteen years old, sitting round, and we know everything. And we end up talking about a united Ireland and why the Union exists, and you have people from both sides of the debate there. Just the very fact for me that they're able to have those kind of discussions, and not be wanting to kick each other's head in, that's what it's about. It's organic, I think, that's the long and the short of it. Friends that I have made, because of where they live, in red-white-and-blue-painted areas, I wouldn't even have dreamt of going into – that's the reality of it, that I've been to see friends, that I have friends at another extreme of my community. That just wouldn't be possible otherwise.

One of Nóra's memories of primary school (the Oakgrove Integrated Primary's first year coincided with her last year before second level) is of the Catholic children being taken out to be prepared for confirmation. She has listened over the years to her mother, the primary school principal, talking about 'the problems and the joys of that sort of religious teaching. Maybe I just think that it should be taken out of the school setting if it could possibly be done outside of school, First Communion and confirmation classes. Because in spite of itself it's divisive.'

While Nóra Murray-Cavanagh is steeped in the ethos of integrated education, Jane Spencer can claim to be the direct inspiration of the pioneer school. As described in Chapter 1, it was the almost-visionary conviction of her father, Tony, that propelled a reluctant All Children Together into supporting Lagan, and then pushed on to set up the next schools four years later. Tony Spencer believed religion should not separate children, and in 1981 he was faced with a personal dilemma concerning the schooling of eleven-year-old Jane.

She is as open and spontaneous as others are solemn and considered. 'I was very aware from the start of how unique the school was. My parents had talked endlessly of how sad they were with the education system in Northern Ireland – and how restricted it was.' She was the youngest of five, and when she turned out to be 'resist-ant' to the eleven-plus, 'paying for a grammar school place was not an option'. The selection procedure pointed her towards Deramore, a secondary school that served a loyalist working-class district. 'The very thought of it made my blood turn to tapioca – I was the one with "Beat me up, I'm a Catholic with an English accent that lives on the Malone Road" stamped on my forehead.

'My dad had spent his life dashing off to meetings and one of them was ACT, an action group. But I'd formed an eleven-year-old's opinion of action groups – that they were quite often anything but. Like that bit in The Life of Brian where they spend their time having meetings about a potential meeting to discuss the next meeting. This, however, is not my father.' Jane Spencer's affectionate thumbnail sketch of her father resembles any number of others. 'There may well be steam coming out of Tony's ears, but the action will be right behind it – he is not a man of pure talk. When my dad came back, with the hugest grin I have to say I have ever seen, and would take a lot of beating even today – saying that he and the ACT gang were going to start up Northern Ireland's first ever "integrated co-ed school" – all I could think was, That means I don't have to go to Deramore.'

After only four to five months of frantic planning, twenty-seven other pupils shared Lagan's first day with Jane: these were 'the Twenty-eight' as a slightly later Lagan pupil says with a dash of mockery today. 'We had police escorts for our first week of school, and had to approach our scout hut through the woods,' Jane Spencer says, but she mentions it very lightly, clearly aware of the major traumas many schoolchildren in Northern Ireland have faced over the years. Pioneering conditions are sometimes idealised in retrospect, and the first days of all the greenfield-site integrated schools are recalled in intricate detail by many founder parents and teachers. A pupil's perspective understandably has none of the wonderment adults recall. From a variety of other comments drawn from Lagan's first ten years of existence, the flavour of a pioneer school comes across strongly, and not at all piously. As the 'sector' hit the twenty-year mark, the less reverent former pupils found the celebrations inclined to be pious and overly ceremonious.

'It was funny recently because Lagan had their service of celebration,' says one of the irreverent. 'And the Twenty-eight were still being deified. I've talked to other people about this – it kind of alienates them, when they had to put up with the same sort of conditions. Nothing to do with the Twenty-eight themselves, but ...'

The conditions that teachers remember with a shudder and the founders list with justifiable pride, marvelling at how far they have since come, were by contrast merely the painful stuff of daily school life for unimpressed, sometimes resentful teenagers. After the initial scouting premises – 'not a scout hut', says a founder, 'it was more than that, that's what it keeps getting called but it was a decent-sized scouting hall' – the tiny but swiftly growing school moved twice in a couple of years, the second time to the hills around Belfast, near the present permanent site. The new site was high up, exposed, far from pleasant.

'We were in the same old building with Forge Primary first,' says another early Lagan pupil who chafes slightly when 'the Twenty-eight' are described almost as lone pioneers. 'And then we were in mobiles up on Church Road. It was pretty miserable. The wind was the worst thing. It ripped up the hill. We were cold much of the time on the top of that hill. Quite a lot of vandalism, I think to do with the environment: ripping a light out of the socket made people feel a bit better or something.'

Like Jane Spencer, he had friends at the established, well-provided grammar schools of south Belfast. Both found themselves hankering in weak moments for the advantages their high-minded parents had withheld from them in the name of an experimental and uncomfortable form of education. Neither was uncomfortable with the mix of religion and class among their schoolmates: it was the frills they missed. Jane was hugely aware, she says, that 'in the grander scheme this was massive and I was very very excited to be part of it. But Lagan as it is now, is a far cry from the Lagan I attended.' She has not seen the college since its tenth anniversary but has looked at their website and was impressed by that in itself, and then by the look on television of today's much-expanded school.

'I have to admit to some mixed feelings about going to a "weird" school, as my friends called it. The joke wore off about going to a "disintegrated" school. Because funds were very limited, and resources were scarce, I felt at times that being part of an experiment, as part of my own secondary education, wasn't very fair. I longed to be part of a school play, or have proper sports teams. I was very envious of friends' chat about language labs and art rooms and computers.' But she cuts ahead to the upturn, and the plus points: 'Castlereagh started taking shape when I was about fourteen, and the facilities greatly improved. We had some cracking people at the school, and the majority of my memories are happy ones.' When she stopped to consider, the only lasting grievance was a tongue-in-cheek one: 'As the pioneering class – we were always the eldest – there was no one to admire, or fancy! A very important factor when you're fifteen!'

But it had been very exciting to be part of something that was so much in the public eye, and she still thought Lagan 'opened my eyes hugely to the world outside'. Jane Spencer remembered with pleasure that with Sheila Greenfield, Brian Lambkin and Doreen

Budd in the first, small premises, the tiny school celebrated Jewish, Hindu and Chinese festivals. There were 'certain individuals' among the teachers who 'more than made up for not having the swanky language labs. Brian Lambkin – with his Moses sandals, and socks! – was an amazing teacher. When we studied the potato famine we learnt some Irish, we visited the Ulster Folk Museum, cooked potatoes, wrote and performed little plays with torn clothes and dirt on our faces. And there was James Burns – a wonderful English teacher, who lit a passion in me for language, books, plays ...'

When she did research on Lagan ten years on, as part of a degree in England, she found the strongest factor in parental choice was 'that it was a very reputable school, and extremely popular amongst children and parents alike. This in itself is a fantastic achievement – the fact that children from all religious persuasions in Northern Ireland are being educated together, and it's no big deal.' It is a point that some later pupils entirely miss, as children of the post-pioneer era.

Remembering small resentments of the time, such as the teasing from others, no longer weighs in the balance against a pride in the scale of present-day integrated education and a lasting awareness of having been part of something remarkable, at a moment of considerable risk. 'I feel we did have to make some sacrifices, among the pioneering pupils, but I can honestly say I don't regret any of it for a second,' Jane Spencer reveals. Not given to large pronouncements, she makes it clear that she does not think of herself as a groundbreaker by nature. But looking back from living and working in England, she also recognises that at eleven she was part of a remarkable development, and that someone she loves deserves more public acknowledgement and credit than he has received:

There's not many people that have contributed to anything so groundbreaking, and I'm very happy that I was involved. I am very proud to have gone to the first integrated school, and I am extremely proud of my father – who fought hammer and tongs, and made himself very unpopular as a consequence. He knows and I know, and his wonderful supportive patient wife knows, what he did to achieve the integrated system that exists in Northern Ireland today, and that's all that matters. And I hope that if it were necessary for me to do something similar for my own children, I would have the same strength and courage of the parents of those twenty-eight first pupils.

6
The Future

The first phase of integrated education may be over, but this is not a sector of systematic, orderly development. Of the forty-seven schools with the title 'integrated', twenty were started from scratch inside the last ten years by small groups of parents and supporters. Lagan College has been venerating its founders and pioneering pupils and celebrating its twentieth birthday: from one perspective it is confident, established and a worthy flagship, from another perhaps losing definition. In the public mind Lagan's twenty years may have suggested an integrated sector that is twenty years old, centrally organised, unified, every school in it equally mature. The truth is somewhat different. There is only the most sketchy of sectors, a teacher claims, adding a description many others recognise or repeat: 'We're all little islands – aren't all schools a bit like that? But when you're started by different people at different times, it adds to the effect.'

There are some connections: a number of integrated schools are admired by their peers, clusters of principals give each other solidarity, and some teachers have strong ties, having moved from one school to another. Teachers, parents and boards of governors elsewhere in the sector feel a lack of support from the longest-established schools and claim these can seem self-centred to a fault. Lagan is resented as a cat that walks alone by many, though often covertly because of its special status. Others retort, with mixed indignation and pride, that former Lagan teachers are now principals, vice-principals and experienced senior staff in a string of newer schools. Natural shake-out and desire for new experience on the part of those who move is undeniably a good thing, say the indignant; perhaps instead a reminder, say the less impressed, that the pool of potential new heads for integrated schools is steadily shrinking. The counter-argument is that applications are growing scarce for the job of principal in the wider educational world in Northern Ireland and in much of England. Many are trying to build the reputations of schools still at the stage of inventing themselves, or are in the middle of working out relationships that will shape their future. There are also a number of situations that can only be described as disasters, usually produced by breakdowns in management or relations between governors and principals.

'GMI [grant-maintained integrated] is such an infant,' said one principal, agonising about the recurrence of disputes between head teachers and boards of governors. She sounded torn between irritation and making the best of it, consoling herself with the idea that what seemed an intractable problem might in fact be more like teething troubles. The adventurous beginning may be twenty years in the past, but in many ways this is still a very new sector, its future course unclear. On the other hand, as a veteran of the first days notes with considerable satisfaction, the concept of a shared space for schoolchildren and the desirability of integration has become part of the furniture. 'The word's inclusive now, that's the thing to be – in politics, socially, and educationally. And we were the first to insist on inclusion, though we called it integration. We're all integrated now, aren't we? Though some of us are more integrated than others.'

For Brian Lambkin, one of the first teachers in Lagan, later its principal and now an academic, but still heavily engaged in support and administrative work for integration, the twenty-year mark is well worth celebrating. 'It began very much as an experiment in the public eye, and it was predicted that the experiment would fail. What we can say confidently now is that it can be done. You can educate Catholics and Protestants and others together, under the same roof, to a satisfactory level. There's no going back from that. And nobody in the conflict arena is advocating that.'

Integrated education is here to stay, a familiar if not entirely predictable part of the landscape. The form it eventually takes and its place in the educational spectrum may not fully emerge for some considerable time. Like the 'mainstream' system, integrated schools are unsure how they will be affected by the outcome of the debate launched by the Burns Report on post-primary education in Northern Ireland, which recommended the end of academic selection for children at eleven. That would be the biggest potential move in education here for more than half a century, said education minister Martin McGuinness, forthrightly setting out his personal loathing of selection and the eleven-plus exam: 'No child should be told at that age that they have failed.'

For many of the strongest voices inside integrated education, the end of selection would be the end of another form of segregation, as Brian Lambkin calls it, and a major opportunity to expand as Northern Ireland's brand leaders in mixed-ability teaching, for all that some schools may have begun to back away from the idea. The Burns debate has taken time to get into gear: in the meantime, recurring questions came up for teachers and organisers, but more urgently, as always, for parents considering whether or not to choose integrated schools. The sharpest dilemma is for those who have made their decision, but whose school of choice cannot take their child.

THE SHAPE OF THINGS TO COME

In March 2002, Saints and Scholars Primary School in Armagh had fifty-three applications for twenty-three places in their Primary One class. The principal, Anne Makin, said that eighteen of the children had older brothers or sisters in the school. A member of staff 'just got her own child in by the skin of her teeth and feels very aggrieved since she was the first assistant teacher appointed'. The scene recurs each year in many of the integrated schools, and teachers find it hard to handle, as Anne Makin made clear. Having no alternative to offer is particularly difficult. Being the chosen alternative, then being unable to provide it, makes oversubscribed schools feel like frauds.

'Most of these young parents have felt for years that they wanted an integrated education for their child and are now finding that it is impossible. They're genuinely distressed,' Anne Makin said, 'and it has been a very upsetting experience dealing with their distress. Some of them said that an integrated education had been in their mind when they decided to have children, and they were in a state of physical shock.' Of the rejected, twenty-one had either phoned or called in subsequently. 'They're mainly young couples with first children, which is why they did not meet the criteria which favour younger siblings and governors' children, for example, plus those who are socially deprived or have July or August birthdays.' Some rejected parents went off immediately to petition politicians and anyone else they could think of. Saints and Scholars was about to tackle NICIE and DENI, while knowing that if they managed to widen their intake, it would only increase concern for nearby schools with falling numbers.

It is a familiar quandary. Integrated education has grown and lasted because of parental demand. Other schools and teachers' unions complain that the integrated sector has damaged mainstream enrolment: the unions have at times claimed that jobs were at risk, to derisive responses from within the integrated sector and outside it. 'It's as if integrated schools had no teachers,' said an angry mid-career teacher, a veteran of controlled schools prior to his present integrated primary. '*We're* union members too. *And* we're employing teachers, we'll be taking on more soon. Wouldn't you think schools might try being honest with themselves about why they're losing numbers?' Like Saints and Scholars, his primary school was, of course, not open to the standard charge that integrated colleges attract those who fail to get into grammar schools and see integration as more socially desirable than the local secondary. But there is of course a similar charge against the primaries: that they too have a certain social standing, smaller classes in many cases lending them charm. What is never admitted by these critics is that integration might be the stand-out attraction.

An academic in education said the unions' attitude to integration 'saddened' him: not a total fan of integration himself, he none the less expected a less partisan approach from trade unionists. But the protectionist reaction is familiar – backs up, hackles up, out of fear of competition as much as of novelty. The anger of those who have written to local papers to protest against projected schools, or who regularly claim that integration is treated favourably and bleeds resources away from the other sectors, is undeflected by the obvious: that integration is a choice, made freely. Continuing demand is the constant the integrated sector lives with and is sustained by, while teachers and others involved in it make a confused and irresolute internal response to a strategy for development largely decided over their heads.

A teacher with experience of the Catholic sector as well as two major integrated schools summed up the road ahead with uncharacteristic doubt: 'I think it's going to enter a new phase with a lot of challenges: the transforming schools are a big problem, but maintaining their ethos and vision in a rapidly changing educational field is going to be just as difficult for the rest.' The use of the distancing word 'their' instead of 'our' might have been an accident, but this was someone who, against form, sounded more cynical than committed. Teaching is tough enough, without anguishing about the direction and prospects for a still-immature sector.

The sector's organising and fundraising bodies exist in a ferment of debate. Does the Burns Report mean opportunity or danger for integration? Should integrated secondary schools cling to their original comprehensive ideals? Do they need a statutory body to coordinate, to be a buffer between teachers and governors and to guide existing, new and transformed schools? Is transformation the likeliest path to growth, and if so, will it dilute integration?

While the argument continues, parents apply for places and are rejected, in Armagh and elsewhere. To take only two examples in different areas, each year dozens are turned away from the heavily oversubscribed second-level New-Bridge College in Loughbrickland, County Down, and Slemish College, Ballymena, County Antrim. The spread of schools has almost reached the point where most areas have a secondary within reach though primary provision lags behind. However, the reach is entirely theoretical for a considerable number of people. Many are trapped economically in segregated housing, and bussing has always been an inadequate solution. Some integrated schools have been able to develop contrary to the exclusively middle-class profile predicted for them because they were forced to locate in mixed, generally more expensive districts. Nevertheless, a considerable number of integrated schools are still more middle class than not. One of the schools that opened in the last six years appears ideally placed to draw children from across the class divide, in addition to attracting a comfortable religious balance. 'No, very middle class,' a non-teaching staff member whispered, discreetly answering an enquiry made out of earshot of the school principal. 'It's not what you'd think. A lot get driven in.' He came to work every day from the nearest working-class district, Catholic and predominantly republican, 'but damn few kids do. From where I live, this is still enemy territory.'

Supposing Northern Ireland should achieve a settled peace in the next ten years, the signs are that social integration will lag well behind political stability. So the challenge for the integrated sector is to continue to meet the muffled demand from people in single-religion communities, but also to recognise the possibility of fixed mindsets gradually dissolving. This calls for serious consideration of communal psychology. Founders and boards of governors sometimes get it wrong, or so teachers in several fairly new schools think.

'Location's always a pain,' one principal confided. 'Obviously if I had the chance to do it again this is not where I would pick.' A normally cheerful and positive teacher looked out at miles of flag-bedecked loyalist housing and groaned. 'Don't know what they were thinking about. Imagine bringing your tender Catholic child here for the first time, or letting them head off here on the bus.' Another described a new school's cautious movement towards reflecting both major traditions in curriculum and ethos. Gaelic football 'will come in time, maybe. The governors are very aware of where the school is sited. They're looking to attract Catholic children, but …' In a number of cases, petitions to politicians and complaints to newspapers have preceded the opening of schools: threats to local businesses thought to be too friendly and/or to the schools themselves have followed, plus sporadic stoning of school buses (though the last is almost a commonplace for many schools across the spectrum).

One school reported proudly and appreciatively on a contrasting experience: a letter to the staff that they interpreted as a welcome from the local loyalist paramilitaries. It asked them to note the absence of flags immediately around the school 'because we did not wish to give offence'. In that particular school's surroundings, awareness of paramilitary approval or at least the absence of hostility instantly lifted spirits. It also encouraged a few to start thinking about the usefulness, and indeed rightness of being situated on what others might think stony ground. The teacher tasked to encourage staff discussion about their own internal conflicts and prejudices thought it the best of omens, and a reinforcement of her own brand of commitment. She said firmly, 'Where's the point in sticking to mixed districts, setting up among nice people or where most of your catchment is middle class? We need to be within reach of the hardest-line places, even if it's uncomfortable.' Then she cited, predictably, the public endorsement of integrated education by loyalist fringe political leader Billy Hutchinson.

The thread of parental choice and parental demand is what many in the sector cling to through confusing and occasionally conflicting developments. People at various levels and in different roles – parents, teachers, governors, organisers or fundraisers – often differ strongly on hopes, fears and strategy, and about the meaning of lessons learned. To one person in a meeting it might seem that the issue capable of causing irreversible damage to integration is the provision for transforming schools. The person in the next seat might well indignantly reject that opinion. Across the aisle another thinks transforming is 'full of possibilities', while the next is less enthusiastic but declares that integration is a process, like transformation. 'It's a journey,' says the deeply religious person at the head of the table, perhaps echoing the favourite metaphor of Sinn Féin's Martin McGuinness about the peace process, as one of those in the integrated world with whom McGuinness the education minister is a hit.

THE ROAD AHEAD

At least as many in the sector are afraid that another journey begun with some ceremony has been quietly abandoned by a considerable proportion of the thirteen schools that voted to transform their status from controlled to integrated and which are meant to satisfy certain criteria. This was originally presented by officials, and also by some in the integrated sector, as the only method by which the ambition to cater for 10 per cent of school enrolment – the declared target of the sector – was likely to be achieved in the forseeable future. There are now major worries: a considerable number think the risks to credibility are too high.

After studying several supposedly transformed schools, one academic came to a devastating conclusion: 'I wonder if any of them are really integrated.' DENI has confirmed that three transforming schools still have a Catholic enrolment of under 10 per cent. Insiders suggest that one of the three is well below 10 per cent, and that several of the ten schools who reached that minimal ambition are only narrowly above it. Research on a wider scale, auditing 'community relations awareness and skills in both grant-maintained integrated (GMI) and controlled integrated (CI) primary schools' was commissioned by NICIE and completed in April 2001. It was then passed to the department of education, who had neither published nor commented on its findings. 'It suggests there's nothing substantially changed about a number of the schools that voted to transform, except the name on the door,' says one insider. 'There are schools playing at this.'

The research, directed by Stuart Marriott of the University of Ulster's School of Education, was in fact downbeat about the ability and training of staff – in several greenfield integrated schools as well as in the transformed schools studied – to confront the divisions in Northern Ireland which strain community relations, and to help pupils deal with them. The study took its title, 'Polite Encounters', from an interview with a principal: 'People run away from controversial issues, run away from them. All they're doing is existing in polite encounters, and children and adults learn more sophisticated ways of hiding their prejudices. That's not what this school should be about.'

But Marriott and his researchers also found a distinction between the schools: 'discussion of both policy and practice did provide a very clear sense that Grant Maintained Integrated (greenfield) schools at least understood the questions – even if the answers were sometimes obscure and always difficult – while in Controlled Integrated (here meaning transforming) schools the questions had very rarely been seriously raised.' One example of different attitudes between the two kinds of school had a GMI chair of governors and a chair of a parents' council similarly claiming that simply being integrated removed the need for community relations work: 'Not that we've fully integrated but we're well on the way. Why aren't you focusing on segregated schools? ... it's there that they need to see the light!'

In two transformed schools teachers were comparatively un-worried about their lack of time for community relations training, and apparently utterly unaware of how monocultural they and their schools sounded: 'we have so few problems here we don't really need training ... because there aren't any problems it tends to get pushed to one side.' One principal remarked that 'I have nothing to do with the other integrated schools' and that 'very few principals of schools like mine' went to meetings of integrated school principals 'because they don't discuss issues relevant to controlled integrated schools ... I went to [their] annual conference last year, I was the only controlled integrated principal there, and they had a talk about flags and emblems which just wasn't relevant to me.'

Marriott concluded that 'some CI schools reflect no credit on the integrated schools movement ... it is unlikely that this will change until transforming schools are required to fulfil more exacting requirements than currently, in order to achieve CI status, and until any additional funding is contingent on meeting realistic community relations' criteria.'

Some in the sector still hope that support and monitoring might bring substantial improvement. 'I feel some sympathy for transforming schools,' says an integrated veteran. 'The teachers I've met feel there's no consultation, they say they feel, What do they want from me, who's going to tell me, where do I find out about this and I've too much work anyhow.' An insider says of the research findings, 'These were controlled schools first, where the principal is god. If the principal has a strong view and is enthusiastic about transformation, it's carried through. If senior management has not grasped what transformation's about, and what needs to be done, then you can take it they're all playing at it.'

But some wonder if DENI and the various bodies in integrated education are also playing games about transformation. The Integrated Education Fund (IEF), set up to raise, manage and allocate money, and NICIE, largely funded by government and charged by it with providing support to integrated schools and parents' groups, have both been supporting transforming schools in various ways for years. DENI has a duty to monitor the process. It is hard to avoid the conclusion that individuals in all three bodies must know which schools are genuinely engaged in a process and which have been 'playing at' transformation. It is also tempting to conclude that 'monitoring', 'audits' and 'surveys' have all been staggered or postponed until the outside agencies think the results might at last be positive. 'Well, no one involved wants to pull the plug,' as a weary observer says. 'What do you expect?' DENI carefully stipulates that transformation 'should be viewed as a series of gradual and definite changes, undertaken with the support of the entire school body ... The ultimate aim is recognition of the school as a fully integrated community.'

Though the 1989 legislation that provided for transformation allows all schools to vote for change except those for children with special needs, no Catholic/maintained school has applied to transform, not that many would have seriously expected a push for transformation from the communally based Catholic sector, where many are neighbourhood schools centred on parish churches with big, and still conformist, congregations. The thirteen are a mixed bunch: four secondary, the rest primary. Their enrolments range from that of the tiny Carnlough Primary to a Lisburn secondary second only to Lagan College in size. The accusation that they voted for transformation as a last desperate effort to avoid closure because of falling numbers might well stand up against some of the smallest primaries. It is obviously off the mark in the case of the 850-strong Fort Hill in Lisburn, which first merged schools for girls and boys, then went for integration.

County Armagh's Brownlow Integrated College, in the middle of ill-starred Craigavon, is generally recognised by the sceptics inside integration as the shining exception, which has 'made the effort' to change its ethos as well as its make-up. But from the start it had advantages many others lacked: the support of striking local characters long established as community leaders (see Chapter 4), and the advocacy of the feminist scholar Chris Moffat who lived not far away and wrote fiery articles for years urging on the transition. It has had an effective principal throughout the process, Errol Lemon, with experience of cross-community work outside school, and it has also had an unusual, not unhelpful history. From early in its life as a controlled secondary, Brownlow High, the staff included several Catholics and the school occasionally had Catholic pupils among children from the British army base nearby, as well as a considerable racial mix by Northern Ireland standards. Two earlier principals tried to build on the school's varied cultures: 'But there was resistance in the staff and among the governors, says one longtime supporter. 'We're not bigots, they said, why do we need Catholic governors and more Catholic teachers?'

The IEF has funded several Brownlow projects, DENI have provided extra funds, and for some time Lagan seconded a Catholic senior teacher to the school. None the less, even with a genuinely enthusiastic senior management team and a determined principal, it seems to have taken the appointment of a Catholic Vice-principal for Integration in 1998, and a more systematic programme of change, to produce convincing transformation.

Effort clearly has to be considerable and concerted. The charge is that a substantial number of transformed schools have made little attempt to change their ethos and atmosphere, the make-up of their boards and the reach of their curriculum. A few in the integrated world hold out against the general pessimism and say that change may well come slowly but will happen eventually. After all, they point out, a number of parents, governors and teachers will have voted against transformation, and will have to be brought along. 'The process is like the peace process, think of it like that,' says one founding figure not otherwise given to talking up transformation. 'There are bound to be slow ships in the convoy.' Another veteran pointed to a school said to have made sizeable moves, after a lapse of several years, towards changing its governors and aspects of its ethos. 'Some teachers there said they would leave rather than teach Catholic kids. Subsequently those teachers said they'd changed their minds. Aren't two unlikely converts better than any number of pushovers?'

Making allowance for schools that have been slow to improve on the small number of Catholics already on their rolls is, in many minds, different from excusing years of apparent inaction. 'X Integrated College? A bad joke,' says an otherwise loyal supporter of promotional campaigns for integration. 'They've changed their name and their uniform and that's about it. It was the town's high school, and I know people there who say X? What's that? Didn't know that was integrated. The bad reputation hasn't changed either.'

Three years into transformation, School X had four Catholic

teachers, then lost two for 'entirely unrelated reasons, and we're wrecked', said the vice-principal tasked to oversee the change. He could see that the two remaining Catholics 'needed to be empowered' by having more Catholic colleagues, though he thought one was 'steely enough'. But no further hirings were likely in the near future. He thought it was 'important to be integrated in a wider sense, to have respect for all – integration of religions is surely just part of that'. The IEF had provided money to improve the school's hall so it could produce more drama and 'engage with the wider community, open up the school. The town is very mixed, you know.'

A moderately sympathetic teacher in the nearest integrated school said patience was only fair. But the process of transformation had only just begun in earnest, she thought. It had taken three years to bed down and 'settle the governors – there were a few who really didn't like it. And I think they're still waiting for the Department or the education board to nominate a Catholic or two. Still, the teachers have been away in the past year for training days with the mediation people and what have you. They're talking about it anyhow.' A less charitable insider observed that the school was struggling to throw off a reputation for thuggishness among the boys, internal bullying, and a level of sectarianism, imported from hard line housing estates, that was obvious in graffiti around the school. She thought the motivation for transformation might well have been that integration would produce more civilised behaviour and a new image. 'In other words, they're trying to dilute an overwhelmingly Protestant, loyalist pupil body with Catholics. Civilising Catholics. You can imagine the governors struggling.' The local Catholic minority might just cooperate in this scenario, she thought, if only because the nearest Catholic secondary was some distance away, but there was no sign of a rush.

The worried and critical know that only a 'holistic' approach to transformation will work: everything tackled together, as part of a well-thought-out strategy. Resistance is remarkably similar in tone from school to school. 'It's always too easy to find reasons for not changing,' a teacher observer says. 'There are always more immediate problems. That's bad for any school, worse for one supposed to be transforming.'

Another observer intrepidly put into words what others jibbed at, declaring, 'When the school tries to address its ethos, it's a question of adding on. So they add, or they talk about adding the Gaelic language, Irish sports, bringing in Catholic teachers. And what happens? Protestants begin to say, What made this a Protestant school? They knew it was Protestant before but there was nothing definite in their heads that said, Here's the thing that makes it Protestant.'

Most objectors to transformation proposals within controlled schools initially insist that these are state schools in which everyone is welcome, already essentially integrated, prevented from being integrated in enrolment only by the stubborn separatism of the Catholic Church and its insistence on having its own schools. The argument mutates, as in Brownlow in the 1980s (see Chapter 4), into complaint that a transformed school will be taken over by Catholics, that Catholic teachers will take Protestant jobs, and that Catholic pupils will fill Protestant places. The Protestant/unionist community will be overborne in some way: transformation means the loss to the community of a Protestant school.

'And then they see pictures of Irish symbols, they hear talk about the Irish language,' says the observer. 'They say, What is there for us. All the movement seems to be towards trying to help Catholics feel more at home in the environment or the teaching staff. They say, *We're* doing all the giving.' The observation mirrors with exactness the complaints of unionists about the relative political positions of the two main communities in the wake of the Good Friday Agreement. Integrated education may hear more such complaints in the next few years. The parallels are uncomfortably obvious, especially to minds already alert to slights real or imagined.

In south Belfast, already beginning to change political colour as Catholics move in and Protestants move out, with a steadily increasing vote for the SDLP and the first signs of a growing Sinn Féin vote, a level of tension is obvious around Finaghy, where a direct road runs from what was once solidly Protestant territory into

Catholic west Belfast. The connecting road has become a barom-
eter: Catholics move steadily closer to the old village of Finaghy,
attacks on homes increase. A proposal in 2001 that the Finaghy
controlled primary should transform, clearly premature, brought
Protestant parents out in scores to protest at an angry meeting.
'Hands off our school,' some shouted. The level of attacks on
Catholic homes went up in the following days, including two on
the homes of teachers from Catholic schools who had nothing to
do with the transformation proposal.

Controlled schools have suffered falling rolls on a far wider scale
than the maintained, Catholic sector, and it is only controlled
schools that have chosen to transform. When integrated schools talk
about local resentment at their intake, they mean they know that
both Catholic and Protestant teachers resent them. Almost always,
it is the Protestant school alone that is threatened by loss of
numbers/teachers/resources.

A maintained school principal may feel slighted by the Catholic
parents who choose the nearby integrated school instead, but will
usually have sizeable classes in any case, with secure teachers. The
majority of school-age children now are Catholic, which some
experts think presages a steady narrowing of the Protestant majority over Catholics in the population as a whole. There are also more
Catholics in controlled primary and voluntary grammar schools
than there are in integrated schools.' Belfast councillor Nigel
Hamilton, of the Reverend Ian Paisley's Democratic Unionist
party told the BBC Radio Ulster *Talkback* programme early in
2002 that he had been approached by parents concerned about the
proposal for the suburban Glengormley Controlled Primary School
to transform to integrated status in September 2003. He had been to
the school himself. 'It's serviced the local Protestant community
within the controlled status, and done a pretty good job. Moving
from one era into another could have a negative impact. Parents are
also concerned that it's part of the manifestation that's taking place
within Glengormley – there seems to be a rolling migration of
nationalism coming in from north Belfast.' To complete the
conspiratorial picture of Catholics everywhere, prospering and

multiplying in their own sector and all the others, some will have noted that it was Catholic parents who took the step that eventually led to the integrated movement.

In the circumstances, resistance to transformation is hardly surprising, nor is the dragging of heels once the process has supposedly been launched. Some people take it as evidence of how essential integrated education is for a more settled and peaceful future. 'Protestants are accustomed to the norm being unionist/British/ Protestant, theirs,' says a teacher and parent of children at integrated schools, born Protestant but married to a Catholic. 'That's where "Ulster says No" comes from. There's no other community. Protestants and unionists are having trouble coming to terms with the peace process, like they had trouble taking nationalist grievance seriously. In part it's bigotry, sure. But it's also unawareness, and unawareness feeds bigotry.'

From this perspective, the transforming schools' slowness to change matches unionist political disarray, and needs as much understanding and help. The teacher adds:

> You have to remember that many don't know any Catholics. Something like the GAA, for example, a huge social phenomenon, that gets the kind of crowds for games that Linfield can only dream about. What does it mean to most Protestants? If one kid was saying to another in class, 'I'm away to Clones for the big game on Sunday,' Gaelic would be just football after a while to the Protestant kid instead of meaning something scary. The Catholic organisation Protestants know most about is the IRA. They don't see the anthem at school prize-giving and pictures of the Queen as Protestant, but they'd be quick to complain if Catholics didn't want them. They'd realise then that their identity was being insulted: the Catholics would suddenly be republicans.

The point was made in a different way by a researcher on integration, who was invited by a friend to a prize-giving in a supposedly transformed school several years down the line from its previous existence. 'They had a local worthy giving the speech, big long screed about the gallant Royal Ulster Constabulary and what the community owed them and the British army. You'd think someone might have said to him, "Here, we're integrated now, bit of sensitivity old chap." But then who would they have to spot that?'

Clearly there is a threat to the credibility of integrated education from transforming schools that have patently not transformed, some of which show little zeal for the prospect. Others chart the varied motives for seeking transformed status, and the extra resources made available which are carefully uncosted in the published literature, but are listed in the 'Information Pack' as 'limited financial assistance'. 'These may include resources to cover the costs of additional teaching staff, development of curriculum materials, books, publicity, training etc.'

Yet only intermittent and muted rage emerges. Why have bona fide supporters and founders and the greenfield schools not raised more of an outcry? Embarrassment is one reason, a wish to be tolerant and encouraging is another. The most powerful pressure might be the demands of marketing and public relations, at the service of a slightly deluded self-interest.

'We have set a target,' one organiser says with a slight touch of desperation, 'that we'll have 10 per cent of the school population in integrated schools by 2008. That means we need to get 35,000 children, more than double our numbers now. It won't be done by greenfield site schools. If every year we had a new grant-maintained school, and the existing ones grew beyond their enrolments and all went to sixth forms, if you include every primary nursery – that would still take us only to about 18 to 19,000. We need to transform existing schools.'

But within minutes the same person was admitting that from the integrated sector's viewpoint there was no adequate or appropriate system to monitor transforming schools. Another, who would usually be considered a well-informed insider, said, 'How the Department is going to define what an integrated school is, beyond their reasonable numbers, their figures for intake, is a mystery.' The comment was sparked in April 2002 by the news that at last DENI inspectors were to formally 'audit' or 'survey' the process of transformation. Both terms were used at various times, though neither was ever defined. Off the record it was admitted that no guidelines had been prepared, much less agreed, after consultation with anyone involved in integrated education. Nor did there appear to be recognition, in either the department or NICIE, that there was something odd about 'auditing' the state of transformation years after transformed status had been awarded.

Brownlow Integrated College, the first to win the change in status, was also the first to be audited – eleven years after its 'transformation'. The school received notice of the audit date two working days before the education minister was interviewed for this book. The minister's office had asked, a month earlier, what areas the interviewer hoped to cover, and was told the non-existent auditing of transforming schools was top of the list. Early in the interview both Mr McGuinness and an attendant official appeared unaware that the audit had now emerged, fortunately timed so the minister did not have to defend a bewildering lack of action.

It was hard to avoid the suspicion of tongues in cheeks, harder still when a flurry of activity followed the survey announcement, with efforts to transmit ideas between DENI and NICIE, and between NICIE and Brownlow, concerning what would be surveyed and how the school might respond. Another swathe of schools were duly notified that they would be next. As the surveys proceeded, word came back of reassurances readily given that there would be no measurement of failure or underperformance. This was hardly necessary. Teachers were certainly nervous and apprehensive about an inspection so close to examinations and the end of the school year. But there was also widespread cynicism, a belief that no one in the schools or in NICIE expected the audit to result in removal of transformed status.

The case against transforming as the fast track to expansion is made with typical verve by one of the founders of the integrated movement. 'There's the moral question – which I think was the old one of "We made schools when our children needed them, we're now obliged to see they are provided as long as anyone wants them." So what if it's expensive? They didn't put money into them for so long. Why can't we start again if need be, doing it from scratch. Why not do the greenfield thing? I don't see why transforming has to be it.' The statement involved a substantial rewriting of history, in the suggestion that the speaker had originally voted to build new schools rather than consolidating Lagan. But the declaration against transformation as the best way forward was fighting talk.

One usually loyal and discreet supporter of the transformation route as the most likely, because cheapest, to achieve a rapid and considerable expansion, insists harsh decisions cannot be ducked any longer. 'I say, at what point do we say this is an experiment that's failed? What I'm told is if we take back the integrated status, we're going to deal such a blow to the local community.' Even for a faithful supporter, this was clearly not a response which effectively silenced criticism, far less disarmed it. Internally divided or simply lacking a centre, and in at least some quarters tempted by the idea of growth however achieved, integrated education may have been too disorganised to ward off a threat to its own long-term credibility.

Help might be at hand, from a new and still surprising element in the situation: Martin McGuinness. Reading between the lines of a diplomatic concern about the genuineness of transformation, a new McGuinness tack is apparent, and is perhaps evidence of a judgement that the process to date has done damage and will do more if not moderated. 'On transformation, I can understand concerns about whether or not this was just people being clever or a genuine commitment to integrated education,' he said. 'There is a responsibility to inspect and see that a genuine effort is being made. Schools will have difficulties, and we can come up with a very rigid line and make life difficult: but that would run against the whole concept of integrated education. Maybe the jury's out on all of that. Maybe concerns can be allayed by continuing support and advice.'

The minister went smoothly on to switch the focus towards an early initiative of his own. On taking office, Mr McGuinness set out to demonstrate even-handedness with an announcement that he had particular sympathy with two groups of parents: those who had set up Irish-medium schools, and those in integrated education. In short order, he lowered viability criteria for both types of school for start-up funding. He did not want to dwell on transformation, he said now. 'It's much more positive to focus on the lowering of the viability criteria. If people can come to the department and produce the numbers, then there's no problem whatsoever in the department granting those schools. There is a real opportunity here for growth. That opportunity has been provided by the lowering of the criteria. That's where the focus needs to be.' As for transformation, that 'remained another possible route – it may not always live up to people's expectations, but we have a duty to continue to encourage people to try and do better.'

Even if education administration could in theory stomach reversing transformations, the first republican minister could not with impunity take integrated status away. All the transforming schools to date have been predominantly Protestant in enrolment and staffing. Mr McGuinness has faced unionist attack for alleged discrimination each time he announces more funding for Catholic or Irish-medium schooling, no matter how justified. Should he reveal hostility to existing transformed schools, he could expect accusations of bigotry and allegations that his support for integration was bogus.

His preference seemed clear nonetheless: that transformation was not a route he would have chosen as a fast-track for integration, and that he recognised the misgivings about it in the rest of the integrated sector. He offered no further clarification, leaving a major question unanswered. With surplus places in the rest of the school system, was the department truly likely in coming years to find funding for a fresh batch of greenfield integrated schools? In reply, Mr McGuinness merely reiterated his insistence that 'the focus should be on the lowering of the criteria'.

INTERNAL RELATIONS

A few in the sector still try to deny that it has an undue proportion of clashes. 'I want this quantified,' a founder-governor responds sharply to the persistent claim that too many principals of integrated schools are burning out too fast. 'I don't believe it's higher than anywhere else,' she adds, pointing reasonably enough to reports on the high rate of stressed principals and other staff throughout Britain. Echoing senior figures in the wider Northern Ireland educational world, she notes that a number of large and prestigious schools have recently had difficulty attracting a wide range of applicants for headships. But one senior educationalist rejects the comparison, gently but firmly: 'It's tough being a head, and getting tougher. But integrated principals are a harassed species. You only have to hear them when they get out into the wider world. They don't pretend.' A second founder–governor scoffs at denials of the scale of the problem: 'If the state or maintained sector had wastage at that level it would be a public scandal. The principals who don't come to grief perhaps have an extra strength.'

A stormy annual general meeting of NICIE in 2001 prompted a 'Governance' working party, which then took more than a year to seek responses from schools, print a code of practice and produce an interim report, promising a final one in October 2002. A somewhat feeble stopgap conclusion was that 'there was unlikely to be a "result"; rather this was the start of a process that should continue to disseminate best practice.' The tone suggested that any recommendations made must contend with the very nature of the integration world.

The working party listed modest 'initial findings':

'Our sector is different in many regards but in three particular ways it was easier to understand why certain problems may arise.

a) Board of Governors are the employing authority
b) Parents start our school and as governors may become over involved in management
c) The ever evolving and rapid changes of our schools and the changes in society.'

Between principals and governors the main issues were 'lack of training/inexperience; lack of understanding of roles and responsibilities and adherence to these (both ways); personality of parties (power struggles); duties outside job description; level of expectations held by both parties, a lack of corporate governance; position of the Governors as an employing authority.'

Though the initial brief was in part to examine 'the handling of disputes between professional staff and Board of Governors', the working party admitted defeat and went for their other, easier instruction, to see how NICIE could encourage good practice. Otherwise they reckoned 'each school would have had to be contacted and Principals and Boards of Governors asked for details or what they saw as the problems and how they dealt with these.' A determinedly upbeat conclusion declared, 'Some of our schools have had problems ... Many of these might have been avoided or reduced if the basis concept of "respect" for all had been better adhered to. Our group wished it to be known that most of our schools have excellent relationships between staff, Board of Governors and parents and that whilst best practice is a laudable aim, we should not take the past problems out of context. It will be inevitable in a new vibrant growing sector requiring multidisciplinary skills that there will be conflict ... We feel this report is a start.'

One disillusioned headteacher makes a stark assessment of the problem: 'There are foundation governors who just won't let go,' she says. Like several others in the sector, she has a husband who is principal of a controlled school. 'He says, *I* couldn't tolerate that.'

The less impassioned are quick to point out that a sizeable percentage of the trouble the integrated sector has seen is because of failings as much among principals as overzealous or possessive foundation governors. The most detached suggest that weaknesses in the composition and training of boards of governors might be compounded by recruitment of insufficiently experienced principals. Across the range of opinion, there is a chorus of insistence that life is hard in general for principals, whether creating schools from scratch or transforming, and for governors. Though more highly charged by tensions particular to integration, it certainly seems that some problems are similar to those in the other sectors. Being principal has never been harder in all kinds of schools, and recruitment and retention of principals is a problem in the education system as a whole. Sitting on a board of governors is different everywhere now, according to a senior education figure:

Across the school sector the roles and responsibilities of governors have changed enormously. If you look at what is now expected of them, their statutory obligations are hugely different from fifteen to twenty years ago. Responsibility for budgets, for example: the thicket of legislation on employment, rules for interviews. In schools of all types there is much more potential for friction between governors and principals. Put at its crudest, it is much more difficult now for governors to say to principals just get on with it, we'll back what you say. Principals now have to manage their governors in a much more proactive, thought-through way. When I started, there was no accountability. I could do what I liked and not account to anyone for it.

The invocation of lost power, with its hint of regret, rings bells with people who have watched fairly shocking scenes unfold in a number of integrated schools. For both principals and governors, battles for control are waged with one side aware how a head teacher's status has declined, while governors in general and integrated governors in particular have a whole new concept of their importance. 'This sense of ownership that governors have, the very strong parental element that there is,' the education figure comments, 'there's a sort of pioneering dimension to it, and think of the sort of person you need to be to be a pioneer. If you look around the integrated sector and talk to integrated principals, there are very few who haven't had a major row.' The problems are already damaging integration's ability to recruit able and experienced principals, some believe.

As with the argument about transforming, monitoring, and the setting of criteria, the need again arises for a statutory body specific to integration. A number of teachers, including several principals, would be happy to see NICIE develop statutory powers. There are several strong counterarguments. One comes from NICIE itself: chief executive Michael Wardlow says it is important for them to retain a degree of independence as lobbyists, an independence they would lose as a statutory body fully funded by government. The others, more passionately, come from teachers, parents and activists at various levels. They say that NICIE itself is part of the problem:

individuals who are now principals have been NICIE workers at various times; moreover, within the integrated movement the web of pioneers, parents and campaigners connected by their shared commitment but also in some cases by marriage and inevitably, close friendship, makes impartiality impossible.

The case that a centralising body is needed is still put strongly, most often by those who fear that integration lacks definition. A number of teachers and parents think there is a danger that the public will see some schools producing an ever more indistinct version of integration, even without the extra blurring and dilution caused by transforming schools. Timidity about introducing even a minimal level of Irish teaching in strongly Protestant districts worries a number, who are also not impressed by the 'sampler' Irish classes offered by a few schools.

In a County Antrim school, a young teacher puzzled over a visit by 'the army to recruit – young boys who came and said how wonderful it was to travel all round the world. There was an uncomfortable feeling among the Catholic staff.' She was not sure the visit fitted with what she understood about integrated education, yet in other ways 'the school's ethos is wonderful: the visits by ministers from all the faiths to speak at assemblies, there's a lovely feeling of belonging, a family feeling'. Others have been taken aback by 'compromises' on the wearing of poppies and other emblems that in effect mean no emblems can be worn. There is a range of approaches to mixed-ability teaching, something founders of the schools thought was central to integration. Many of the secondary schools, perhaps most, find it too difficult to teach children of widely different ability in the same class. The alternatives used include taking different groups out of a form for a number of subjects, teaching them together for others, and full-scale streaming, as has been Lagan's practice for years past.

'I think we've backed away from some uncomfortable decisions,' a widely respected teacher says. Another remarks sadly that the schools are 'islands, like all schools are to some extent. But I thought we would be different.' The pressure for academic results has been intense, many say. A new brand of education in traditional, results-orientated Northern Ireland was bound to feel that strain, and the race to be recognised as viable, to win funding and respectability, has had a cost. 'I think for some of us the integration thing has been pushed on to the backburner,' said a veteran in a County Tyrone school. 'It's inevitable once something becomes part of the system. Parents are sending their kids now because we're seen as good schools, giving a regular secondary education. They're not sending them primarily for integration, so the pressure isn't coming from them. When I started, it would have been.'

The role that many would still like filled is a combination of energiser, keeper of the flame, impartial arbitrator in disputes, and well-resourced, skilled adviser. Some think no one body could or should do all these things. Many are ambivalent about who should fill the arbitration role: DENI, NICIE, or education and library boards (ELBs). For the moment, the suggestion is that integrated schools feel that to a degree they fall into the cracks, and that they are the prime responsibility of one body only – an under-resourced and overstretched group, which is to some far away in Belfast: NICIE. In March 2002, Michael Wardlow complained bitterly that the NICIE budget for the year had just arrived: £425,000 the previous year had improved to only £431,000, leaving staffing at 'two and a half development officers and not the three that were recommended – by external consultants and agreed with the Department – simply to stand still'.

Because of their piecemeal development, integrated schools were set up with a variety of management structures and became the responsibility of different bodies at different times: a few funded by ELBs, most eventually by DENI. But since the ELBs have never had more than one or two integrated schools at a time to deal with, there is no general board expertise in dealing with integration, and there is a mixture of official attitudes towards the greenfield schools. One widely shared opinion is 'they think we're funny people', though others report helpfulness. Some by contrast think there might be the beginnings of official pride in integration, a disposition as the trend has grown for DENI and the ELBs to send foreign visitors to see 'our' local integrated school.

In any case, the future of the five boards which divide responsibilities geographically for the whole of Northern Ireland is in some doubt. Devolution has put in hand a long-promised review of all administrative structures, which are widely regarded as heavy with duplication and overstaffing. Martin McGuinness was happy in early 2002 to talk about his 'liking' for integrated education, and his intention to see that integrated schools received any help they needed. He was resolutely unspecific, citing the review, about the possibilities of expanding NICIE's remit in a way that would set it up as a new and additional type of ELB or CCMS.

POWER AND INFLUENCE

In some minds, the organisations set up to assist or promote integration are fairly irrelevant. The idea was the important thing, and to the many vindicated true believers, it is an idea whose timing was clearly impeccable. 'I think we're moving from the time of the visionaries to the suits,' says the worried veteran, struggling to keep teaching at the same pitch in what clearly seem less idealistic circumstances. 'Visionaries might not be the best at directing,' she admitted. 'The problem is keeping the ethos, and parent governors, governors, new people coming in may not have the same vision. Staff development is going to be really crucial. I'm not sure who's going to be responsible for that.' Integrated principals and teachers train with others in schemes run by DENI, ELBs and the Regional Training Unit, but can these offer the kind of advice needed? After a thoughtful discussion, the worried teacher seemed to take some comfort from a reflection that had nothing to do with organisation, and everything to do with commitment: 'In the end it'll probably come down to individuals in each school keeping the flame.'

One teacher's worry that each school 'is reinventing the wheel' is for another an inevitable and vital process in which different groups of teachers work out their own ways of dealing with difference. For the most optimistic, a strong sectoral identity is neither necessary nor desirable. A considerable number say they think the most lasting and significant impact of integrated schools on education as a whole might be a leavening of the segregated system. 'What we want to happen,' said one pioneer, 'is surely what seems to have happened already: in other words Catholic and Protestant schools have become a bit more like each other.'

The evidence offered is the Catholic Church's recent move to present their schools as welcoming to all children, but also the small number of grammar schools once largely Protestant, now increasingly mixed and choosing to describe themselves as 'multi-denominational'. Neither is a major advance but they convince optimists that a move is under way. Interest in the development of shared Christian or interchurch schools is more widespread. The possibility mooted by the Burns Report of grouping schools throughout Northern Ireland into collegiates, which might well put a premium on each collegiate having a school that could offer integration to match specialists in other areas, is also to some minds a glowing potential opportunity. Yet another tendency sees the possibility, still some distance away, of secular schools with emphases familiar in the present integrated world: a welcome for all classes, races, and beliefs, strong parental involvement, and some kind of mixed-ability teaching.

In March 1985, an *Irish Times* story with the headline 'Three integrated schools planned', quoted spokesman for the Belfast Charitable Trust for Integrated Education, Joe Mulvenna: 'We don't think we are going to solve the whole Northern Ireland problem by having our children educated together. We aren't making any big claims like that. We just think it would be a step towards developing understanding between the two communities and breaking down some of the prejudices we all have. It's not only the children we hope to bring together, it's the parents too.' The mixture of modesty and breathtaking ambition was characteristic of that era – energy-giving fuel for that first leap forward. In October of the same year, Tony Spencer said, 'Our ambition is to have one third of all school places in Belfast integrated by the year 2000.'

The grand Spencer plan may have fallen some way short but the face of education has changed forever with the establishment of a robust if still small integrated sector, and in new young parents there are signs that the initial fervour survives. Doubts and fears about transformation have only fed the instinct among parents to start from scratch, say some activists. With help from NICIE, groups of parents are investigating and building local support for three new primary schools, one to open in 2003, a second in 2004. Meanwhile, two controlled schools have successfully balloted their parents on the transformation process, and some in a third are discussing the possibility. One early supporter looks at the scene and remarks, 'Some of the same issues are still around today so what's the strategy for development? Is it to create a broader interest in the community? Is that the right way? Or should it be to target certain places for integrated schools? I just wonder what's the meaning of integrated education to somebody living in the middle of Ballymurphy in Catholic west Belfast. You'd have to be mighty committed. Does integrated housing have to come first after all?' Another time-worn enthusiast and early governor takes the long view, and is more upbeat: 'I'm a historian, so I'm a sceptic. I went into it hopeful but sceptical. I emerged less sceptical, and still hopeful.'

Anne Murray of Oakgrove Primary in L'Derry is a principal who first started thinking about the possibility of integrated schools as a young teacher. Although a Catholic, she deliberately began her career in a controlled school because she wanted to break through the predictable path laid out for her. She sees the future as full of hope, though not at all certain, and she is not at all disposed to think integrated schools have segregation on the run. But at a time when some are worrying that integration has lost definition, and is in danger of becoming less distinctive the more schools establish themselves as solid educational institutions, she sees their task as clearcut: 'It isn't enough when we get children into school to let them sit side by side and say ah, some day you'll find out that one beside you is a Catholic or a Protestant. We have to be upfront about the education that we give them and say this is what makes you the person you are and so on.'

She also thinks the future might bring more division, this time usefully: 'As secularisation grows, will we end up with a section of integrated schools which are joint church schools? Maybe the Christian Churches will circle the wagons and say let's get together on this, as they've started to do in other countries like Australia, for example. We might wind up with a big sector of integrated schools and within that there'll be a division, and it'll be joint church and secular. The other two sectors, Protestant and Catholic, will shrink, and this one will grow and then divide.' She adds with a cheeky grin: 'Sure if it's in Ireland it has to divide.'

Whatever the concerns about organisation, structure and inbuilt tendencies to confrontation, the conviction and determination of many in integrated education is undiminished. At bottom, few see an alternative to what they are about, except acceptance of a status quo that in fact is itself in flux. As society in Northern Ireland likewise adjusts to a new political order, or struggles to come to terms with it, the place of integrated education in the society struggling to emerge is for many undeniable if yet to be defined.

For what has been the bigger community over much of Northern Ireland's history, lack of understanding and knowledge of the minority in their midst has hindered political development. Protestants and Catholics have lived side by side without understanding even when they refrain from fighting each other. One integrated education stalwart, a Protestant by upbringing says, 'Segregation has damaged Protestants, unionists, more than Catholic nationalists. It was their state, and many still don't credit the reality of Irish, nationalist culture as anything but a deliberate affront to them, a form of opposition. All of this is fed by separate schooling. I think a lot regard Irishness as a bogus political stance, because they only know Catholics as political figures, not as friends to talk to openly. It's why they're so slow to come to terms with a new deal based on parity of esteem. They're not ready or not able to swing round. It's why they're bogged down in the foothills of "culture", symbolism, marching.' To this way of thinking, developed through an adult lifetime dominated by the Troubles, it seems unanswerable that open and honest schooling of a mutually respectful nature and a childhood shared, would surely have helped many to take a broader perspective.

How can it be bad for Protestant and Catholic children to be educated together? The state of politics and the slow progress of the peace process illustrate how separation, misunderstanding and mistrust make adjustment difficult, to the point of pain for some. By comparison with the bloodstained recent past there is now peace of a fractious kind, but not yet reconciliation by a long way. In the eyes of many dedicated people, brave parents, teachers, and their selfless encouragers who have built a thriving alternative to the segregated schools of Northern Ireland, the development of schools which bring children together from sundered communities may be a political necessity if there is to be a better future for all.

Appendix 1

Northern Ireland's Integrated Schools

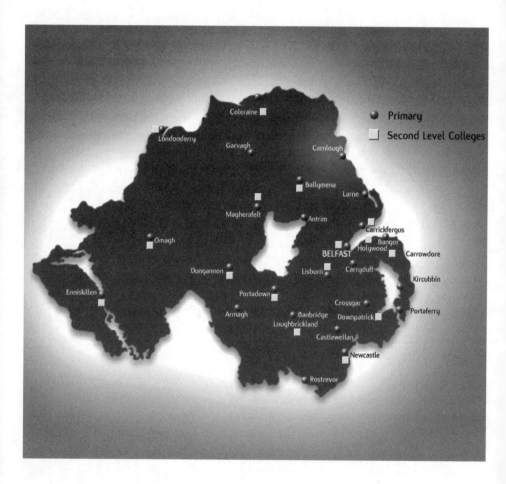

Appendix 2

Enrolment in Integrated Schools, 1998–2002

				LEVEL	1998	1999	2000	2001	CHANGE
1	1981	Lagan IC	Belfast E	secondary	966	964	967	1015	49
2	1985	Hazelwood IC	Belfast N	secondary	675	685	691	718	43
3	1985	Forge CIPS	Belfast S	primary	220	214	220	228	8
4	1985	Hazelwood IPS★	Belfast N	primary	395	402	395	461	66
5	1986	All Children's CIPS	Newcastle	primary	189	204	202	227	38
6	1987	Mill Strand IPS★	Portrush	primary	221	217	219	210	-11
7	1987	Bridge IPS	Banbridge	primary	370	384	394	393	23
8	1988	Windmill IPS★	Dungannon	primary	152	175	185	216	64
9	1989	Braidside IPS★	Ballymena	primary	225	251	254	290	65
10	1989	Enniskillen IPS★	Enniskillen	primary	213	220	207	238	25
11	1990	Omagh IPS★	Omagh	primary	184	184	180	225	41
12	1990	Portadown IPS★	Portadown	primary	200	201	195	221	21
13	1991	Brownlow CIC (trans.)	Craigavon	secondary	364	364	362	365	1
14	1991	Corran IPS★	Larne	primary	149	142	141	189	40
15	1991	Carhill CIPS (trans.)	Garvagh	primary	45	50	45	47	2
16	1991	Oakgrove IPS★	L'Derry	primary	400	391	394	440	40
17	1992	Oakgrove IC	L'Derry	secondary	719	755	768	780	61
18	1992	Acorn IPS★	Carrickfergus	primary	198	198	205	229	31
19	1993	Saints and Scholars IPS★	Armagh	primary	166	193	191	229	63
20	1993	Lough View Primary	Belfast SE	primary	185	213	241	267	82
21	1993	Cranmore Primary	Belfast S	primary	143	157	160	162	19
22	1994	Erne IC	Enniskillen	secondary	366	376	391	384	18
23	1994	Shimna IC	Newcastle	secondary	355	412	459	460	105
24	1995	Integrated College Dungannon	Dungannon	secondary	306	401	433	468	162
25	1995	Cedar IPS	Crossgar	primary	115	135	156	198	83
26	1995	Drumragh IC	Omagh	secondary	424	530	536	532	108

				LEVEL	1998	1999	2000	2001	CHANGE
27	1995	New–Bridge IC	Loughbrickland	secondary	322	387	434	456	134
28	1995	Portaferry CIPS (trans.)	Portaferry	primary	55	65	66	87	32
29	1996	Hilden CIPS (trans.)	Lambeg	primary	66	66	73	72	6
30	1996	North Coast IC	Coleraine	secondary	249	327	419	450	201
31	1996	Oakwood IPS★	Derriaghy	primary	100	113	135	178	78
32	1996	Rathenraw CIPS (trans.)	Antrim	primary	105	103	101	102	-3
33	1996	Slemish IC	Ballymena	secondary	266	389	485	563	297
34	1997	Annsborough CIPS (trans.)	Castlewellan	primary	46	51	44	45	-1
35	1997	Ulidia IC	Carrickfergus	secondary	150	230	329	398	248
36	1997	Strangford IC	Carrowdore	secondary	150	239	328	420	270
37	1997	Malone IC	Belfast S	secondary	257	388	513	650	393
38	1998	Bangor Central CIPS (trans.)	Bangor	primary	482	479	499	483	1
39	1998	Kircubbin CIPS (trans.)	Kircubbin	primary	90	100	98	108	18
40	1998	Kilbroney CIPS (trans.)	Rostrevor	primary	57	64	63	70	13
41	1998	Priory CIC (trans.)	Holywood	secondary	395	392	437	450	55
42	1998	Down Academy CIC (trans.)	Downpatrick	secondary	300	269	293	276	-24
43	1998	Forthill CIC (trans.)	Lisburn	secondary	755	813	843	893	138
44	1999	Spires IPS	Magherafelt	primary		58	96	121	63
45	2000	Millennium IPS★	Belfast S	primary			10	55	45
46	2001	Carnlough CIPS (trans.)	Carnlough	primary				28	28
47	2002	Sperrin IC	Magherafelt	secondary					55
		★includes pre-school unit							
		TOTAL			11,790	12,951	13,857	15,069	

NOTES

Information taken from NICIE annual reports

By September 2002 there were 47 integrated schools (18 secondary and 29 primary).

(trans.) = transformed schools

Differences between DENI and NICIE figures in the appendices are due to fluctuating enrolment figures in the course of a school year.

★includes pre-school unit

Appendix 3

Statistical Overview

Religious Affiliations of Integrated School Pupils, 2001–2002

Protestant	6,645
Catholic	6,047
Other	2,288
Total	14,980

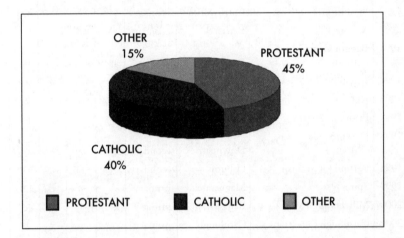

Pupils at Integrated Schools as Proportion of Total School Population

2001–2002	Total nursery, primary and post-primary population 340,635
2001–2002	Integrated population 14,980 (4.5%)

Source: Department of Education for Northern Ireland

Appendix 4

Changes in the DENI Viability Criteria for Integrated Schools

1990   An intake of 15 pupils in primary schools and 60 pupils in post-primary schools with a minimum overall enrolment of 100 pupils in primary schools and 300 in secondary schools

1996   An opening enrolment for all new primary schools of 25 pupils with a long-term enrolment in the range of 150–175 pupils, and for new post-primary schools an opening enrolment of 100 with a long-term enrolment of 500 pupils

1998   Minimum opening enrolment for post-primary schools of 80 and long-term enrolment in Forms 1–5 of 400 pupils

2000   To be recognised as viable, an intake of 15 for new schools in Belfast and Derry and of 12 for developments elsewhere. When schools achieve intakes of 20 in Belfast and Derry and 15 elsewhere, they become eligible for capital funding.

2001   Intake of 50 in Year Eight (first year) for post-primary schools

Index